THYSSEN-BORNEMISZA COLLECTION

MONASTERY OF PEDRALBES

Fernando Marías
Consuelo Luca de Tena

The act of creation in itself transcends the individual to become a vehicle of universal communication,and this is why I believe that as far as possible works of art should be accessible to everyone.

Baron Hans Heinrich Thyssen-Bornemisza de Kaszon, 1992

© Publication: Fundación Colección Thyssen-Bornemisza, 1994
© Photographs
Fundación Colección Thyssen-Bornemisza, 1994
The Thyssen-Bornemisza Collection, 1994
© Text:
Fernando Marías y Consuelo Luca de Tena, 1994
© Translation:
Hans R. Hoetink and Viveca Bachrach

I.S.B.N.: 84-88045-89-1
Deposíto Legal: M-46.470-1998

Layout of the book and cover design:
Daniel de Labra

THYSSEN-BORNEMISZA COLLECTION
Monastery of Pedralbes
Bajada del Monasterio, 9
08034 Barcelona
Tel.: 280 14 34 Fax: 204 16 01

Contents

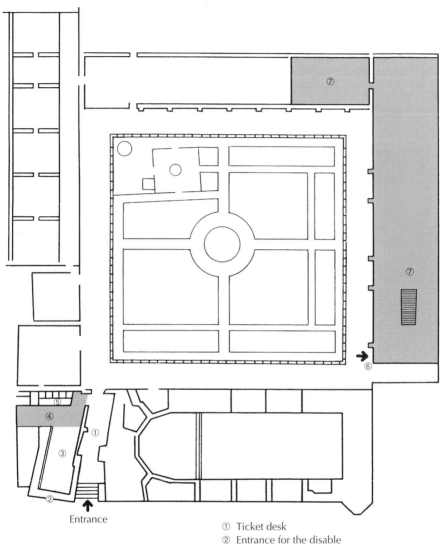

Entrance

① Ticket desk
② Entrance for the disable
③ Cloakroom
④ Museum shop
⑤ Toilet
⑥ Entrance and lifts to Thyssen-Bornemisza
⑦ Thyssen-Bornemisza Gallery

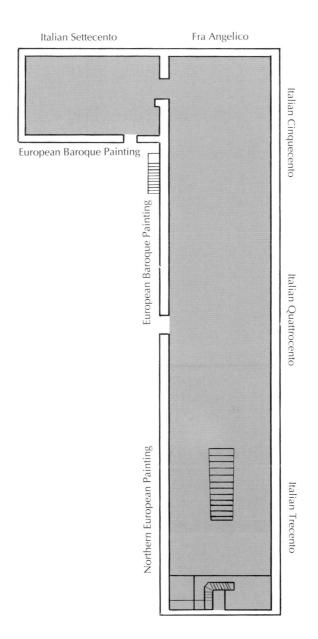

Italian Settecento

Fra Angelico

European Baroque Painting

European Baroque Painting

Northern European Painting

Italian Cinquecento

Italian Quattrocento

Italian Trecento

Introduction

The works of art that are on view in the Pedralbes monastery in Barcelona are part of the collection built up by the Thyssen-Bornemisza family over the course of two generations. Started in the third decade of this century by Baron Heinrich, it was considerably enriched by the present Baron Thyssen-Bornemisza, Hans Heinrich.

This collection, which contains about eight hundred paintings, was initially lent to the Spanish state for a period of nine and a half years and was then permanently acquired through an agreement signed on the 21st of June of 1993. Although the majority of the collection is exhibited in the Villahermosa Palace in Madrid, an important part of it — mainly consisting of panels and canvases that cover the period from the end of the thirteenth century until the second half of the eighteenth century — is on view in Barcelona.

Thanks to the generosity of the initial owners, the number of works in the collection has been expanded by an additional loan of paintings, sculptures and other works of art that enrich and adorn the exhibited collection. Some of the medieval paintings and sculptures that are shown in Pedralbes are part of this loan, alongside the seventy paintings belonging to the Spanish state.

The setting chosen in Barcelona, the beautiful monument that is the royal monastery of Santa María de Pedralbes, is one of the most important buildings of the Catalan Gothic and was chosen by the municipal government of Barcelona to house this part of the Collection. The monastery was founded and endowed for Franciscan nuns in 1325 by lady Elisenda de Montcada (1293-1364), the fourth wife of James II. She retired there after his death and was burried there later. The tomb that today is heavily restored represents her both as queen and nun by means of two reclining figures. The monastic church, with a single nave, chapels between the buttresses and an elegant octagonal bell tower, was begun in 1326. This date coincides with the construction of other remarkable buildings in Barcelona, such as the parish churches of Santa María del Pino (1322) and Santa María del Mar (1328).

The ground floor of its sober and majestic cloister gives way to the chapel of Saint Michael. Its walls were decorated with scenes from the lives of the Virgin and Christ, and were painted in oil after 1346 by Ferrer Bassa (†ca. 1348) and his son Arnau Bassa, who introduced the style of the Italian Trecento in the princedom. Thus, this chapel forms one of the most important items of Spanish art since the fourteenth century.

The Collection, which shares the building with the community of nuns and with the Monastery Museum, occupies two rooms in the northern part of the Pedralbes complex: the former bedroom and the Queens Hall, which have been suitably restored and adapted by the architects Pere López Iñigo and Josep Maria Julià to exhibit the Collection.

On the one hand the selection of paintings and sculptures in the Pedralbes collection intents to reaffirm the link between Italian and Catalan mediaeval painting — so clear in the chapel of Saint Michael. On the other hand the Collection's section of medieaval art from other European countries hopes to contribute to the knowledge and enjoyment of the artistic culture that came to such high achievements in the hands of Catalan artists. It has also been the intention to show the works that are most representative of the specific interests of the Thyssen-Bornemisza family as art collectors, from the Italian Renaissance — in which the painting by Fra Angelico "The Virgin of Humility" stands out for its supreme quality — and its Central-European counterpart up to the Northern and Italian Baroque of the seventeenth and eighteenth century. Lastly, a pair of Spanish seventeenth-century canvases has been added on at the end in order to account for —albeit testimonially — the importance of the Spanish artistic legacy within modern European painting.

NB: The technical information on each work has been reduced to a minimum in the catalogue. When an artist represented in the Collection is mentioned for the first time his dates of birth and death are given in parenthesis after his name. In some cases the names of the works cited in the text are abbreviated. When they are mentioned their catalogue number is given in the form "Cat.x". The letter A which sometimes appears in these mentions, e.g. Cat. A x, designates the work belonging to the additional loan mentioned above. The complete information on the work, the date of execution, technique, dimensions and catalogue number are given in the list of works published at the end of the book.

I Medieval Sculpture

The Collection's sculptures form an interesting reflection of the diverse European production in the Early Middle Ages and offer a general overview of the main currents that coexisted and succeeded each other during the Gothic period in France, England and Italy.

From this latter country procedes *The Dead Christ* (Cat. S102), in polychromed poplar wood and dated in the mid-thirteenth century. From this region and period other similar examples are preserved (such as the sculpture at the Cathedral of Tivoli), although of greater emotional solemnity and effect. An almost life-size Christ that is executed according to the anatomical and proportional treatment typical of the period — his body is covered only by a dark loin-cloth that reaches to his knees — is pictured in the moment of the lowering of the cross. As a result it has been assumed that it formed part of a group of scenographical figures that today is lost, and in which it was placed between the disengaged figures of the Virgin, St John the Evangelist, who are depicted in an emotional and anticipating attitude, and of Joseph of Arimatea and Nicodemus, who were about to receive the dead body in their arms. If the sparse remains of the polychrome that represents the blood of the wounds in the side, hands and feet were a reliable reflection of its original state, one could think that the intention of its creation was to affect the faithful viewer of the group with the inert mass of the falling body, with its serene beauty and its unconscious embracing gesture, rather than with the pathos captured by the composition of the figure or the emphasis on the graphical testimonies of Christ's physical suffering. This Christ, which stylistically is situated half-way between the late-Romanesque sculptural tradition of Benedetto Antelami and that of the naturalistic renovation of Nicola Pisano, represents a moment in Italian sculpture in which the realism of the image in terms of volume and anatomy is emphasized through the elimination of linear conventions in the description of the loin-cloth. Nevertheless, this style does not achieve the compository complexity, the naturalistic movement and the detail that is introduced by the school of Pisano.

The Seated Prophet (Cat. S96) comes from Northern France (given its relation to works by Senlis and Mantes) and could be dated at the end of the twelfth century. It can be considered a good example of the formal means employed in previous decades by the Romanesque sculptors. The bearded figure, wearing a cap and shown in a pensative posture, supports his chin with his right hand while the paper roll that he holds in his left hand falls on his right leg in a con-

S102. *The Dead Christ*, c. 1230 - 1250
Polychromed poplar. Height: 174 cm.

ventional way in order to balance the main fold of his robe, which together form a cross. Beyond the simple, frontalized and symmetrical composition the form is defined by the linear play of parallel lines which are the results of the work of a dented chisel on limestone, contributing to the rythmical and reiterated liveliness of the sculpture's surfaces.

Despite having a similar geographical origin — namely Northern France — *Head of a Prophet* (Cat. S95), made of lime-stone and dated in the second half of the thirteenth century, presents a very different atmosphere. This work, that can be linked to the works from the workshop at the cathedral of Reims, shows the renovating elements of the French Gothic sculpture of the first half of the thirteenth century. The linear conventions have given way to an interaction between the internal volume and the plastically treated surface, while the curvilinear play of the graphical design has been substituted by the organic corporal movement, the lack of expressiveness by an elegant serenity. Naturalism has attacked the fortress of the descriptive conventions of

S95. *Head of a Prophet,* 1250 - 1300
Limestone. Height: 38 cm.

S96. *Seated Prophet,*
c. 1180 - 1185
Limestone. Height: 125 cm.

14

S97. *Virgin and Child*, c. 1250 - 1275
Sandstone. Height: 181 cm.

art and converts the reliefs on three-dimensional forms into sculptures in rounded shapes.

The monumental sandstone figure of *The Virgin and Child* (c. 1250-1275; Cat. S97) has also been placed in this period and region (it procedes from the village of Sionviller in the Lorraine, in the district of Meurthe-et-Moselle, where it was found in a niche in the street). It formed a sequence to similar figures in the main entrance of the western façade of the Reims Cathedral and to the *Golden Virgin* of the Amiens Cathedral, with which it has more in common because of its greater rigidity and a more similar treatment of the drapes. In this group the Virgin supports the Child, who turns towards her, on her left arm without showing him to the viewer or establishing a visual dialogue with him. Christ grabs the bulbous brooch that holds together Maria's cloak — blue with golden ornaments, like the Child's tunic and in accordance with the rest of the polychrome that has been conserved, although maybe not with the original — on top of a red dress. The crowned and smiling, apparently pensive Virgin directs her gaze above Christ and supports the Child's foot, which is clearly shown to the viewer, with her right hand as if to indicate that the mother's carresses at a given time lead to injury and, with it, to the completion of his redeeming mission, in conformity with a widely propagated iconography.

The also monumental and beautiful sandstone image of *The Virgin and Child with Moses and the Burning Bush* (Cat. S98), which dates from the beginning of the fourteenth century and is maybe from Burgundy, corresponds to a subsequent stage. The naturalism of the image and the action has been accentuated; the Virgin supports the Child on her hip in a natural manner while the latter tries to reach what his mother holds out at him and holds a small bird in his left hand, which assumes a symbolical meaning in its incapacity to escape in the same way as the Child must assume his mission. Nevertheless, a wide, conventional curve organizes the composition and the set of drapes of the Child's tunic and of the Virgin's cloak, which she holds over her right arm, acquire a merely decorative function. The intelligent and complex composition is completed in the lower part by the figures of Moses and the bramble bush — skillfully worked with a trepan — that burns without getting charred and which, thus, symbolizes the eternal virginity of Maria, even after Christ's birth. A praying Moses, who is of humble dimensions and wears clothes of the period, has taken his shoes off in a gesture of respect, lea-

S98. *Virgin and Child with Moses and the Burning Bush*, 1310 - 1330
Limestone. Height: 155 cm.

ving a pair of splendid and gentleman-like high riding-boots at his feet instead of the more modest biblical sandals.

The French polychromed wood sculpture *The Virgin and Child* (Cat. S99), which may procede from the Mosel Valley and is dated in the first half of the fourteenth century, may seem much more conventional and sacred. The inexpressive and rigid Virgin, dressed in a blue tunic and a red and golden cloak, holds a laughing and forcefully moving Child in an unlikely manner, bearing witness to the propagation and popularization of the great creations of the cathedrals' and courts' workshops.

The stony French figure of *The Knight* (Cat. S100), from the middle of the fifteenth century, ought to be placed in this environment. With a bun on his head and dressed in a short doublet that shows the arms and legs covered by an armor and holding a shield, the figure may have formed part of a polychrome funeral group in the Sluteran tradition, as an attendant accompanying the *pleurants* that formed the fu-

S99. *Virgin and Child*, 1300 - 1350
Polychromed wood. Height: 101 cm.

neral escort of a nobleman, whose arms he would be holding. Despite its greater simplicity, the roundness of its volumes that were later defined by polychrome and the facial expression of contained grief would endorse its latest stylistic origins and its function.

The latest of the Collection's sculptures is a small English alabaster (probably proceding from Nottingham and dated in the second half of the fifteenth century), *The Assumption of the Virgin* (Cat. S101). Beneath God the Father who is flanked by two angel musicians, the Virgin ascends on the background of a "mandorla" and is supported by four cherubs with eyes in their wings. Underneath, on the left, appears the figure of St Thomas wearing Maria's belt; according to the apocryphal story of the death of the Virgin, it produced the second act of incredibility of the apostle, who was said to have doubted the ascension. Miraculously transported from India, where he was working as an architect, he arrived in time to receive the belt in his own hands, thrown down by the Virgin in her ascension. Produced as individual panels or forming small altarpieces in a series for internal consumption or for export, *The Ascension* may have formed part of one of these, dedicated to Maria's Joys, whose devotional function weighed heavier than the artistic interest of their creator.

S100. *Standing warrior,* c. 1450
White stone, with remains of polychromy. Height: 86 cm.

S101. *The Assumption of the Virgin,* 1450 - 1500
Alabaster. Height: 40.7 cm.

II The Italian Trecento

The long history of the art that came out of the Medieval centers of the Byzantine Empire, its official character and its homogeneity had created a high level of craftmanship and an extensive repertoire of formal conventions and of iconographic recipes that for a long time were essential for any great pictorial or musical enterprise that was undertaken in Italy. While in several places on the Italian peninsula the great future centers of Renaissance art were being formed, the *Greek manner* still constituted a common language against which the great creators of the renovation in the Trecento reacted: Giotto di Bondone, who translated the previous style to an *Italian manner*, and Duccio di Buonisegna, who gave a new modernizing impulse to the translation without completely renouncing its legacy.

The two small panels of *The Crucifixion* and *The Final Judgement* (c. 1290; Cat. A.895 y A.894) could be good examples of the situation previous the the irruption of these two guiding lights. They have been attributed to an anonymous Master of the Dotto Chapel (active from 1290 to 1315), painter of the now disappeared frescos in the Dotto Chapel of the church of the Eremitani in Padua. After at first having been catalogued as works by the Florentine Cimabue its creator was later considered to be Venetian because of the Byzantine elements that dominate his work — the linear definition of the forms, the lights that mark the superficial relief of some flat figures, the feelings based more on movement than on facial expression — and seemed to exclude any other possible origin. The two panels are thought to be part of a portable dyptich formed by twelve scenes from the life of Christ and to which another three panels belonged that are in other collections. In both panels the gold forms the rich and abstract background against which the artist depicts the essential elements that, in a synthetic way, clarify both the represented episode and the elements that, with clear symbolical implications and without any attempt at narrative or spatial coherence, indicate the meaning of the picture.

In the first panel the crucified Christ, who has a conventional anatomy and composition, has just died. A diminished kneeling figure whose scale demonstrates the lack of coherence of a representation that takes hierarchy more into account than visual logic, presents this work's donor, a Franciscan monk, to us. The earth opens at his feet, revealing the skull of Adam. In the background a shallow representation of the city of Jerusalem rises up, using the inverted perspective. Behind St John the Evangelist and through a parapet the Temple shows us the veil that according to the Gospel was torn up from side to side and that symbolizes the end of the Law

A 895. **Master of the Dotto Chapel**
The Crucifixion, c. 1290
Tempera on panel. 17 x 18.2 cm.

A 894. **Master of the Dotto Chapel**
The Last Judgement, c. 1290
Tempera on panel. 17 x 18.3 cm.

21

of Moses. Behind the Virgin a centralized and dome-shaped structure — reminding of the Dome of la Roca — could refer to the New Church.

In the second panel the *Second Parousy* is shown to us in which the motives of the prophet Isaiah's and St John the evangelist's apocalyptic visions are mingled. On the frontal plane, on the right, an angel reaches out for the sky "in the way a book is rolled up", with a sun "as black as a mane" and a moon that is "as red as blood" (Apocalypse, 6, 12-14), a Byzantine motive that forms a simple but impressive transcription of the biblical text. On the left a second angel with his trumpet announces the end of time, waking up a group of characters that are closed in by a kind of arch. He stands within green surroundings, the meaning of which could be searched for in the words of the prophet (Isaiah, 24, 21-23), who describes a moon that would blush and the sun would be ashamed on the day that Yahweh descents to visit "the kings of the earth ... shut up in a dungeon, confined in a prison", but which could also represent the cho-

248. **Master of Forlì**
The Deposition, c. 1300-1305
Tempera on panel. 19.7 x 13.3 cm.

321. **Pietro da Rimini**
The Nativity and Episodes from Christ's infancy, c. 1330
Tempera on panel. 17.2 x 19.7 cm.

sen ones. The center is occupied by the figure of Christ during his second coming and who appears in the form of a Judge, showing his wounds and with his feet on the Book. He stands in the middle of a "mandorla" between two angels that support the symbols of his Passion, such as the Son of the Man of the Gospel of St Matthew, resplendent with "... a rainbow...resembling an emerald vision" (Apocalypse, 4, 3).

Another example of the presence of Byzantine painting is the heavily restored *The Deposition* (c. 1300; Cat. 248), attributed to the Master of Forlì, an artist who had his formation around Venice in order to later work in the Romagna. Again we find the golden background that dignifies the work's appearance and closes its space, and the minimal elements of a theatrical *attrezzo* that endows this picture, depicting a story in which the figures do not yet desist a conventional treatment, with a certain amount of scenographical verisimilitude. However, it heralds an important change in the depiction of the Gospel: there are no more symbols, but only facts. The basic information from the story of the New Testament is adorned with a wealth of details from other literary sources, such as the Meditations of the Pseudo Buenaventura that are very descriptive and visual: the task of pulling out the nails and the lowering of the inert body, the fervour of the embraces and kisses that the female saints and St John lavish upon it. The group of figures, however stereotyped they are, form an expressive scene of human pain and suffering in which the reiteration of some of these on successive steps produces the impression of a chorus that finds its peak in the union of the faces of the Virgin and her Son, the real center of the scene, and which accentuates the painting's dramatism. This scene has been considered part of a tryptich of a Life of the Virgin of which other panels are kept in several collections.

A new change along the lines of a naturalistic representation of the episodes — both in a physical and emotional sense — is represented in the Collection by a very small panel that is clearly indebted to Giotto's art and has been attributed to Pietro da Rimini, who worked in the area of Venice and the Marches around 1315-1335. These *Episodes from Christ's Infancy* (Cat. 321) are considered part of a tryptich of which other panels (The Presentation, The Maries and the Sepulchre, and Noli Me Tangere) are conserved. The initial episodes in the life of Christ (The Birth, The First Bath of the Child by the Midwives, The Announcement to the Shephards and the Magi) are combined in one single scene. This practice is frequent in painting at the time, but here the task is resolved with particular skill thanks to the play of gestures and looks that cross with each other between the characters, joining them in vivid dialogues and avoiding a weakening of the picture's unity as a result of the dispersion of the motifs. Moreover, the looks and gestures are natural and expressive and endow the figures with an intense human reality that makes one forget the forcefully conventional iconography. Although we can find direct precedents to almost every fragment of the painting, some details still reveal a fresh and original observation of nature (the childish restlessness with which the Child turns to his mother and at the same time reaches out his arms towards the Magi; the animated conversation that these are maintaining; the tenderness and dedication with which the midwife holds out the towel). Despite the fact that, amongst the four panels that are supposed to be part of the same dyptich, this one is precisely the least Giottoesque, the mark of the great Florentine painter is beyond doubt present in the way in which the depiction of the holy episodes is humanized and in which a feeling of naturalness is created by means of the inclusion of elements that are not strictly necessary for the comprehension of an illustrated text. Also, the suggestion of volume in the figures and in the pictorial space — which is still defined with conventional forms and through which the former can easily move — contributed to the translation of the stereotypical formulas of the foreign greek into the naturalistic vulgar language.

This renovating process is even more palpable in the work of Taddeo Gaddi (active from 1300 to 1336), a Florentine from a famous family of

152. **Taddeo Gaddi**
Nativity, c. 1325
Tempera on panel. 35.5 x 37 cm.

artists and who was Giotto's favourite disciple and his assistant during many years. Although he lacked the brilliant power of his master, Gaddi standardized the practice of the Giotto's style, assimilating his narrative clarity and the clean distribution of space. His figures lack the round plasticity of Giotto's, but maintain his dignified soberness and his poise. In his *Nativity* (c. 1325; Cat. 152) we can see the clear order of the parallel planes, the deliberate search for perpendicular lines that give stability to the composition, and the balanced distribution of the volumes that frame that which is essential. The Virgin dresses the Child — a motif that serves well to impart the sentimental tone he looks for. St Joseph, who sits somewhat aside, seems overwhelmed by the worries caused by the events. The two midwives Noemi and Salomé that appear on the right, do not appear in the Gospel and form part of the repertoire of motifs that the painter extracted from the Apocryphal Gospel, which are very rich in episodes and anecdotes on Christ's infancy and the Virgin's life. Here they are shown to us when one tries to convince the other of the event's prodigious character as related by the Protogospel of St Jacob. One of them shows a sign of astonishment while the other supports her incredulous companion. On the left the scene used to continue with an Annunciation to the Shepherds. The panel has been cut off, but one can still see the stick on which one of them was supporting himself, a sheep and an angel that turns towards them after having abandoned the group that shows us the Child in the entrance, a skillful way to connect two episodes.

Gaddi uses other formulas to increase the feeling of naturalism of the scene. Despite the convention of the golden background that represents the sky, and the apparent contradiction in the resolution of the lights that define the volume of the figures, the treatment of the atmospheric shades seems to indicate the painter's desire to place the narration in nocturnal darkness, the hour at which the Birth would have taken place.

Bernardo Daddi (active from 1312-1348) was also a disciple and assistant of Giotto. His *Madonna and Child* (c. 1340-1345; Cat. 122) is highly representative of his personal style and of the direction taken by Florentine painting after Giotto. The son of Daddo di Simone, Bernardo was active in Florence and died of the Black Death. He developed the more lyrical and sentimental aspects of his master's work, soon letting himself be seduced by the decorative and anecdotal tendencies of Siennese art, and specializing in devotional pictures, above all of the Madonna and Child.

The popularity of private devotion had created an enourmous demand for this type of painting that was not narrative but purely pictorial. Pictures of the saints and also scenes extracted from the Passion, such as the Man of Suffering, the Pietà and the dead Christ supported by angels — themes stripped of all action that tried to provoke an intense emotional reaction in the viewer that would precipitate oration — became very frequent. The favourite picture was that of the Madonna. The *glykofilousa* Byzantine Virgin was renewed in a thousand forms; the Virgin would loose the meditative quality that characterized her Byzantine representations and which held the symbolical meaning of a premonition of the Passion, in order to devote herself decidedly to the tenderness towards her Son. These sweet virgins were not missing in any bourgeois household and specifically left the Daddi workshop in great quantities, on panels richly decorated with a profusion of gold molds, as valuable and desirable objects. In these there is always a play between the mother and child, who at times holds a small bird or receives a flower and who moves with an infantile vitality that, doubtlessly, caused an intimate and content recognition, especially amongst female devoted clients.

122. **Bernardo Daddi**
Madonna and Child, c. 1340-1345
Tempera on panel. 84 x 54.8 cm.

In this panel the only trace of Giotto's style is the compact profile, although here it no longer tries to transform volume. The elimination of space by means of the golden background results in a lack of interest for volume, and the figure is presented to us in a delicate bas-relief. A delicate modelling softens the features and gives the faces a dreamy expression. This Madonna and Child was at first triangular, but was converted into a rectangle. It is thought to be the central piece of a polyptich that had wings with St John the Evangelist, St Jacob the Elder, St John the Baptist and a Saintly Bishop, which are now dispersed over several collections.

The work of Niccolò di Tommaso (active 1346-1376) represents a step backwards. He had his formation in Florence with Maso di Banco and later in the workshop of Nardo di Cione. He was mainly active in Tuscany and, above all, in the city of Pistoia. This *Madonna and Child with Six Saints* (c. 1362-1367; Cat. 303) follows the example of his master Nardo di Cione's Madonna, now in the Historical Society of New York, very closely. Here the Virgin holds the Child, who has a goldfinch in his left hand while he blesses with his right hand, in her arms. On the left of the throned Virgin and below an angel appears St John the Baptist, who is pointing at Christ, a saintly deacon martyr and St Batholomew with his knife. On the right are St Anthony the Abbot, St Nicholas and the Archangel Michael. As this one, Nardo's Virgin appears seated but without it being clear where, as she is cut off on the background of a brocade drapery that is prolongued as a carpet (although there is no shading not foreshortening nor any other indication that the material is in a vertical position behind the Virgin and horizontal beneath her). In this painting the supposed carpet ends in a socle, which can be interpreted as part of a throne, while in the case of Nardo's Madonna the spatial ambiguity is even more extreme. In it, the Virgin wears a dark blue cloak with ermine on its lapels, which cross on her lap and in a conventional manner fix her seated position.

The Virgin shows us the Child in a ceremonial way that is closer to the old Byzantine *hodegetrías* than to the sweet Madonnas that we have seen. The Child does not play nor does he seek the caresses of his Mother. Rather, he blesses in a serious posture and the Virgin once again takes on the abstract and melancholical expression of the Byzantine Madonnas. The bird in the Child's hand is no toy but a symbol of the Passion and the Resurrection. Niccolò also copied this from his example, but in Nardo's painting its symbolical meaning is much clearer as the Child looks at it seriously, thus inviting us to follow his meditation. On both sides of the Virgin superpose the figures of the saints and the angels without the smallest attempt from the painter to keep any proportions in relation to the Virgin nor to define the space in which these figures are placed. Their forms overlap as two-dimensional silhouettes and their rendering is so basic that it barely produces a sense of volume. All these characteristics may seem the archaisms of a retardant artist but, curiously enough, they are even more pronounced in Nardo di Cione's work, a more important artist. In fact, in Florentine and Siennese painting of the 1350's and 1360's a return to modes of representation from before Giotto's transformations has been observed. There is a renunciation of three-dimensionality and a return to a strict hierarchy in the size of figures according to their real im-

303. **Niccolò di Tommaso**
Madonna and Child with six Saints, c. 1362-1367
Tempera on panel. 87 x 39 cm.

portance, a renunciation of the personal relation with the viewer, a return to more symbolical iconographic themes and to rituals in the treatment of episodes, a concentration of the sacred rather than the human, frontality and rigidity rather than natural poses and movements. There is also a greater enrichment of the paintings by means of gold paints and brocades, and a preference for more intense colours. All these "regressions" can be explained as a consequence of the profound social and spiritual changes that took place in Florence and Sienna, the Italian cities with the largest artistic activities during the first half of the century, after the Black Death that devastated them in 1348. The atmosphere of insecurity that followed this disaster left the most sentimental form of piety without meaning, while the intimate relationships with the saints gave way once more to a consecrated distancing from the divine. At the right time a more popular clientèle would have imposed a taste for easier stylistic forms, given their more traditional way of perceiving images, and a greater effect of material wealth. The small panel, which conserves its old frame, formed part of a tryptich.

The *Madonna and Child with two Angels* (c.1374; Cat. A.896) by Barnaba da Modena (Barnaba di Ottonello Agocchiari, Modena, c. 1328-c. 1386) can also be placed within this line of preference for material richness and sumptuous effects. This painter probably trained in his native city and in Bologna while he worked mainly in Genova and Pisa. The style of his youth in some ways is similar to that of the main painters of the Bologna School at the time, Tommaso da Modena and Vitale da Bologna. In his adulthood he produced numerous devotional pictures like this one, in a retardant style and with a conscious recuperation of Byzantine formalistics and an exquisite execution. This Madonna, signed with the inscription *"BANABAS DA MUTINA PINXIT IN JANUA"*, excellently represents the characteristics of his art. The gold is applied profusely and not as an abstract background for the figure but in order to present very specific material qualities. In the Virgin's coat and dress it serves to repeatedly depict the fine folds of the materials. If chrysography was a usual recourse in Byzantine painting, where it surely arose as an imitation of enamel effects, it was less frequent in Italy even though it was used with the same intention of adding richness to the painting and endowing it with a proper light. Some colours, such as ultramarine and vermilion (exactly the usual colours of the Virgin's tunic and cloak) were difficult to shade and raise due to their intensity and profundity. Especially the ultramarine, which was obtained from the extremely expensive lapis lazuli and in itself containted extraordinary beauty, would loose

A 896. **Barnaba da Modena**
Madonna and Child with two Angels, c. 1374
Tempera and gold on panel. 51.5 x 37.6 cm.

part of its splendor or turn dark when mixed with white. Drawing a network of lines with the gold one could manage to depict a fold and enrichen a monochrome surface rather than suggest volume, without risking the precious colour's purity. The cloth of the background contributes to the sumptuousness of the effect thanks to the vivid combination of red and gold and to the fine shading that makes the surface vibrate, thus producing a sense of dense texture.

Italy knew a long and important textile tradition and its products, which include Oriental, Chinese, Persian and Islamic motifs, exerted a powerful attraction on many painters, who did not only copy these patterns in the painted materials of their paintings, but also often were fascinated by their shiny surfaces and their bright colouring.

In Italian Trecento painting this current competed with the more intellectual and "progessive" preoccupation with the problems of three-dimensionality. Works like this one represent a more conservative stream that was founded on the solid base of various learned crafts. The craftmen's workhops were real industrial centers where all crafts were combined, and the quality, fine execution and material beauty of the products was the most important for a large part of their clientèle. In the intimate semi-darkness of some private oratory, in the indecisive candle-light, the virgins of artists like Barnaba da Modena, excessively decorated in gold, would radiate a subdued splendor that was like an emanation of divinity.

Cenni di Francesco (active 1369-1415), can also be placed in this tendency. He had his formation in the circle of Andrea Orcagna and was an assistant to Giovanni di Biondo in his youth. This panel, *Madonna of Humility with the Eternal Father in Glory, the Dove of the Holy Spirit and the Twelve Apostles* (c. 1375-1380; Cat. 85), shows characteristics of Orcagna's work, such as the rigid symmetry and the hierarchic and ceremonious presentation of the figures. They are grouped without any proportion between them and without any attempt by the painter to give them the three-dimensional space which that rigid rendering seems to demand. We find ourselves in front of an ideal space in which a curious iconographical combination is found: the so-called Madonna of Humility is seated on the floor on a hassock, reaching a conventional breast to the Child. In the majority of the paintings with this theme both Christ and his mother look directly at the viewer, forcing the Child into a complicated, twisted pose.

This theme was first used in Sienna in the circle of Simone Martini, surely as a sign of independence from the Virgin of the Nativity. The earliest versions showed the Virgin in profile, with her head inclined and hovering over the Child with her body. These paintings were immensely popular even outside Sienna, maybe because the exaltation of Christ's humanness and the virtues of humility corresponded perfectly with the preachings of the Franciscans and the Dominicans as well as with popular devotion, and perhaps also because of the formalistic aptness with which the motif developed from its origins. Its most interesting development occurred in Florence as a consequence of the tendence towards more pious interpretations and towards less narrative and more symbolic contents: gradually the Virgin would be presented seated in a more frontal pose and with a more erect back. Behind her a rich cloth of honour would be stretched while the angels accompanied her and her hassock was lifted unto a dais. In this way the Virgin of Humility paradoxically was merged with Regina Coelis. Numerous examples reflect the repeated use of this interpretation of the Virgin as the most exalted, and simultaneously the most humble of creatures. This theme of humility was sometimes also combined with the Incarnation (as in this case), with God the Father (in the form of Christ) sending the Holy Spirit upon the Virgin — as in some Annunciations. The present version is one of the most peculiar as it also incorporates elements from the Ascension, such as the presence of the twelve Apostles, the angelic choirs and the appearance of Christ

85. Cenni di Francesco di Ser Cenni
The Madonna of Humility, c. 1375-1380
Tempera on panel. 76.6 x 51.2 cm.

within a "mandorla" that is closed by two ovals of cherubs and angels.

With *The Coronation of the Virgin with Four Angels* (c. 1380-1390; Cat. 3) by Giovanni (di Salamone di Ser Albertino) da Bologna (active 1377-1390), another popular theme of the devotion of Mary appears. It describes the Golden Legend by alluding to a verse of the Song of Songs ("Come, my wife, so I can crown you"). This theme spread after the middle of the twelfth century, coinciding with the high point in the devotion of Mary and ended up dominating the main façades of French cathedrals. The creator of this small panel was a painter and goldsmith and worked in Treviso, Venice and, probably, in Padua. In this city Altichiero da Verona has refreshened Giotto's teachings, which we see reflected in his simple and powerful volumes that are lifted into relief by means of a

3. **Giovanni da Bologna**
The Coronation of the Virgin and four Angels, c. 1380-1390
Tempera on panel. 45 x 21.7 cm.

strong shading of the flesh and in the subdued lighting in the materials, in the soberness of his tone and in his efficient creation of a space that has a minimum of elements — such as the succinct architecture of the throne behind which four angels hover in prayer and the gable of which seems to be topped by a symbolical lily.

Andrea di Bartolo (active c. 1380 - Sienna, 1428) was trained and worked in Sienna and traveled to Venice and maybe to Dalmatia. His *Christ on the Way to Calvary* (c. 1415-1420; Cat. 6) formed part of an altarpiece predella that now is dispersed. It is a direct transcription with barely any stylistic novelties of the version by Simone Martini (Louvre, Paris), which in turn was inspired by Duccio. The meeting between Christ

6. Andrea di Bartolo
The Way to Calvary, c. 1415-1420
Tempera on panel. 54.5 x 49 cm.

45. Bicci di Lorenzo
Christ on the Cross with the Virgin and Saint John, c. 1430
Tempera on panel. 75.5 x 31.4 cm.

and his mother shows a symbolic rendering of the city of Jerusalem and does not appear in the Gospel. The "Meditation" by Pseudo Buenaventura, on the other hand, do narrate this event in a luxuriously detailed and intensely emotional manner. It concerns the Virgin's anguished course — after taking a shortcut — from the crowd to the meeting with her son on a roadcross. The dramatic moment of the wordless exchanging of looks between the two, while they are immerged in an anonymous crowd of people, was what captivated the imagination of the painters and what set the definite formula for depicting this scene.

Bicci di Lorenzo (Florence, 1373-1452) inherited and transmitted his art within his family's workshop. His ample production of frescoes and panels attest to his established position and his solid clientèle. He conserved a late-Gothical style well into the fifteenth century, and always wor-

46. **Bicci di Lorenzo**
Announcing Angel, c. 1430
Tempera on panel. 69.3 x 30.8 cm.

47. **Bicci di Lorenzo**
Annunciate Virgin, c. 1430
Tempera on panel. 69 x 31.9 cm.

ked with a dignified level of quality and a pleasing elegance. The arrival in Florence of Gentile da Fabriano, whose good manners evoked a long-lasting fascination in Bicci, had a decisive and consolidating influence on his style. His *Annunciation and Crucifixion* (c. 1430; Cat. 45-47) are good examples of this pleasant style that is devoid of drama and conforms to the standards of good taste. In the Annunciation the Archangel appears flying above some clouds in accordance with the prototype that was introduced by Ambrogio Lorenzetti. But what in that example was an almost violent invasion of the angel that provoked a frightened reaction in Mary here is a serene and correct presentation of her more dignified interpretation that favours both Gabriel and God. The ecclesiastic clothing of the Archangel can be brought back to the same prototype, although here it is reduced to a stole. The lily she carries in her hand has its origin in the sceptre ending in a lily flower that is Gabriel's emblem. In the Crucifixion the Virgin and St John the Evangelist maintain a very strict composure without giving in to excessive demonstrations of suffering, while the pelican that wounds itself at the breast in order to feed his children symbolically represents Christ's charitable sacrifice. The three panels must have formed the crown of a polyptich.

The tendency to recuperate certain Giottoesque formulas was taken up by the Camaldulite friar of the Florentine Santa Maria degli Angeli, Lorenzo Monaco (active c. 1370-1426, in that same century called Giovanni di Pietro), whose monastic situation defined his name and who combined a fluid line and the sweetness of his native Sienna with the heritage of the Master of Bondone. His large tempura panel *Madonna and Child Enthroned with Six Angels* (c. 1415-1420; Cat. 227) — the central painting of a tryptich — represents the transformation in a ascetic sense of the Siennese international Gothic, which he submitted to a process of de-ornamentation that went accompanied by an intensification of the religious emotionality, which he endowed with a more voluminous treatment. His application of simple colours in subtly harmonious combinations and the greater freedom of movement of the angels contribute to this effect. The angels support censers at the front while they bunch together in order to watch upon the Mother and Child with moved and emotional gestures. The contrasting colour scheme of the clothes or the furniture reinforce the sense of volume and space that culminate in the robust figure of Christ, who blesses us and, like Mary, turns his eyes towards the viewer. The devotional quality of the painting remains intact despite the ample naturalistic interests. The rigid symmetry and the lack of proportion between the figures intensify the painting's consecrated character. Although to a lesser extent, the decorative quality of the linear drawing that curves the borders of the Virgin's cloak, forming a smooth bodily throne for the Child, also remains, as well as the courtly sense of elegance of the secondary figures, who maintain their arched traditional design.

This interweaving of Gothical traditions and devotional functions that are closely felt by a religious person like Lorenzo Monaco could only superficially incorporate Giotto's teachings, into which an artist like Masaccio during those same years blew a new life and tone. A new sense of the secular, introduced by Humanism, and new means put at the disposal of art through the scientific vision of nature formed the basis of the Renaissance tendency that in the end swept away the attempts to reconcile the traditions that already belonged to the past.

227. Lorenzo Monaco
Madonna and Child enthroned with six Angels, c. 1415-1420
Tempera on panel. 147 x 82 cm.

III The Italian Quattrocento

Starting at the beginning of the fifteenth century and coming to an end around 1600, Italian Renaissance art caused an extreme change in the conception and production of artistic objects. With the study of nature, the ruins of classical Antiquity and the contemporary practices as a point of departure, quattrocento painting created a new figurative system that tried to align the visual experience of its products with human perception of reality, while the feeling of finding oneself in front of a piece of fiction was not yet lost. Painters in this period invented a new, ordered and proportioned way of representing the reality of space and of the bodies and physical objects in it, as well as of the perspective, which in accordance with the interests of these new times added a scientific dimension to artesan practices. They also attempted to endow their work with the prestige already enjoyed by literature, history and poetry, thus elevating their artifacts into a new category that was closer to that of scholarly liberal artists than to that of the mechanics and artesan craftsmen of the Middle Ages.

Nevertheless, in some artistic centers that were far removed from innovative Florence or from other centers of high intellectual standard, the renovation could only be very gradual. Sometimes such places even resisted the extemely humanized and cultured art that subverted the categories and interests that had been conferred to art through tradition. For this reason a number of "pseudo-Renaissance" methods — as opposed to those of the true Renaissance — can be identified. A profound investigation of these styles and their linking to other cultural and religious interests still remain to be executed.

The great painting of the Florentine Renaissance, which reached its second peak — after 1434 — during the time of Cosimo de' Medici the Elder, is represented in the Collection by the large tempera on panel *The Madonna of Humility* (c. 1433-1435; Cat. 7) by Giovanni di Pietro da Fiesole, better known as Fra Angelico (Fiesole, c. 1390 - Rome, 1455). He is the Dominican artist who led the secular humanist art of Masaccio into the road of Christian Humanism, as if he had tried to integrate the most modern culture into the Thomist tradition of the order of the Preachers, to which he belonged, and the official Church.

The Virgin of Humility (as the "foundation of the spiritual edifice" according to St Thomas Aquinas) was the favourite theme of the mendicant orders. The image was essential in the movement of strict observance of the Franciscans, and recurred frequently both in Italian literature — associating this version of the Virgin with sublimity — and painting during that period. When we look at the image's evolution

7. Fra Angelico
The Madonna of Humility, c. 1433-1435
Tempera on panel. 98.6 x 49.2 cm.

from its Siennese creation to its Florentine assimilation, where the Virgin is elevated on a podium and depicted in a frontal, erect and dignified posture, with rich materials and where the motif of the breast-feeding was suppressed, Fra Angelico gave it another impulse. On the one hand, he emphasized the symbolical attributes, but at the same time placed them in a highly humanized discourse. The Child gives his Mother a white lily that symbolizes Mary's purity and that reappears in the vase which, in order to balance the composition, she is made to hold. It rises above three red and white roses, symbols that could refer to the her identity as a "thornless rose" as well as to Christ's future suffering. On the other hand, despite Lorenzo Monaco's and Gentile da Fabriano's influence and his friendly and ornamental linearity, the painter managed to endow his figures with powerful volume (his materials give away the body they cover, the colours define the forms) and his devotional or narrative images with a great spatial coherence, and reveal the assimilation of the new artistic directives. His fi,gure's passive beauty remains intact, but at the same time a new humanized feeling, rather than heroic courage, has become part of their saintliness. The emotional relationship with the viewer, who is faced with ideal creatures instead of with simple images, is intensified. Giorgio Vassari relates that Fra Angelico painted without ever correcting or changing anything and that he was convinced of being able to count on divine inspiration. His works transmit a serene view of a beautiful and ordered world that unfolds itself in absolute harmony of form and colour under the eyes of God, and his art in this way allows for man's salvation from his world.

The spreading of Florentine Renaissance art through more peripheral areas took place due to the many contacts that existed between artists, through influences and even the importation of art works. The local traditions were solid and the interests of both religious and courtly clients did not necessarily coincide with those of the Tuscan innovations, not even with their less revolutionary versions. In the main provincial centers a phenomenon of active rather than passive symbiosis took place, propitiating some decisive advances according to the diverse functions that were assigned to the images and their particular concerns. In the Ferrara of the Este family this symbiotic process of adaptation was realized by three painters: Cosmè Tura, Francesco del Cossa and Ercole de' Roberti.

The pair of small tempera panels of *St Claire* — with the book of the foundation of the Franciscan's feminine branch — and of the virginal and wise princess *St Catherine* — martyrized on the wheel — (ca.

103. **Francesco del Cossa**
Saint Claire, c. 1470-1472
Tempera on panel. 27 x 8 cm.

104. **Francesco del Cossa**
Saint Catherine, c. 1470-1472
Tempera on panel. 27 x 8 cm.

1470-1472: Cat. 103 and 104), are by Francesco del Cossa (Ferrara, 1436-1478). They seem to have belonged to the pedestals of the impressive, orderless and monumental *Annunciation* of the old Bolognese church of La Osservanza (Dresden Pinacotheca). This placing would justify the molding of the consoles on which both female saints rest their feet, as these play with the illusion of volume escaping from the painted surface. The sense of relief employed by the painter brings the figures out from the space of their niches, which are in a precarious and worrisome state of preservation. Their hollowness and the treatment of light in them emphasize their volumetric quality even more.

Traces of the painting style and the clear lighting of Piero della Francesca and of Donatello and Andrea Mantegna's art — which he was able to see in Padua — can be recognized in the treatment of volume and space in Francesco del Cossa's work. The somewhat hard atmospheres of the heads, which are outlined by means of profiles of light, the complicated scheme of materials on St Catherine and the material sense of the artificial objects bring echoes of the metallic and excentric art of Tura to mind. The elegant and somewhat mundane air of this figure allows us to imagine the painter working on the decorative and courtly frescoes at the Palazzo Schifanoia in Ferrara between the pagan divinities and esoteric astrological representations — the profane high point in his art.

The art of Giovanni (di Pier Matteo) Boccati (Camerino, the Marches, c. 1410-1480) seems more archaic and retardant, and can be placed in what Federico Zeri called the *Pseudo-Rinascimento* or the dark Renaissance. He was active in Perugia, his native Camerino and Urbino, but was probably trained in this latter center, as can be deduced from the close likeness of his style to that of other painters that in this city developed their activity around the same time: Benedetto Bonfiglio (of whom a lovely *Annunciation* is preserved in the Thyssen Collection) and Bartolomeo Caporali. Both are provincial painters who, however, show a very fine and delicate taste and who assimilated the sharp lighting of Domenico Veneziano and the focus on ornamentation and the fragile and puppet-like figures of Benozzo Gozzoli, who also worked in Urbino. Later on Bocatti came into contact with one of the most interesting and suggestive circles of the times, Padua, where Squarcione was teaching and where Mantegna commenced his revolutionary work in the Scrovegni Chapel of the Eremitani. Bocatti then moved on to Urbino and was one of the first artists to work for Federico da Montefeltro; in the ducal palace he painted a room with large figures of warriors in

50. **Giovanni Boccati**
Saint Sabinus conversing with Saint Benedict, 1473
Oil on panel. 27 x 35.9 cm.

which he tried to merge real and fictitious space in his desire to apply what he had learned from Mantegna's frescoes. Nevertheless, the possibility for fiction and the perspective control of the space and architecture seem to have been seriously limited, as can be judged from the clear incorrectness of his handling demonstrated by other works of his, such as the one in the Collection.

The small oil panel *St Sabinus Conversing with St Benedict* (1473; Cat. 50) depicts the consultation by the bishop of Canosa of the Benedictine monk in Montecassino, in front of the entrance in Rome of the Gothic King Totila, and formed part of the predella of an altarpiece painted for the San Savino Chapel in Orvieto. This work included a main panel with a throned Madonna with Child and Saints (Budapest) and depicted another three scenes from Christ's life: the blind St Sabinus offers proof of his powers by recognizing Totila in a banquet; the archdeacon Vindemius tries to poison the monk; and the death of the saint. Bocatti's interests seem to have centered on an animated or serene depiction of the hagiographical episodes that he was commissioned to execute. He framed them in unlikely spaces that, however, were full of the charm of the immediate or poetry of the landscape's nature, in which the every-day details were shown with a craftman's interest for the description of material life and exert attraction upon us for their basic, naive and almost popular quality. In this way the clarity of the conversational gestures, as well as the minute definition of the figures with the innumerable folds of their clothes and the very detailed depiction of objects, become more meaningful.

The paradoxical ambivalence of style — between a rationalized construction and imaginative escapades, between an adherence to the scientific Renaissance and the departures towards the irrational — reaches one of its peaks in the art of Francesco di Giorgio Martini (Sienna, 1439-1501), one of the most many-sided and contradictory artist of the late Quattrocento. He was a disciple of the Vecchietta (Lorenzo di Pietro) in Sienna, which had become Tuscany's second most important artistic center. He had his training as a painter and sculptor, even though his most important activity was that of architect and engineer — above all in hydraulic engineering and fortification — in Sienna, Milano, Naples and the court of Federico da Montefeltro in Urbino. He left behind an important and innovative treatise in which he dealt with these fields. Painting took on a secondary place in his activities and his style shows a close likeness to that of his fellow disciple and workshop companion, Neroccio di Bartolomeo. The archaic and delicate, almost female tone of this military engineer's painting is surprising, as is his capricious use of perspective — providing for unstable pictures in which the objects are deformed in an arbitrary way by their forced foreshortening. He was a consummate architectural draftsman and constructed very rigorous and stable structures. His fragile and mannered physical types in complicated dancer's poses are very characteristical, as well as those of his sculptural reliefs, in which they are set with the aplomb of their three-dimensional bodies and their logically organized anatomy.

Despite the apparent simplicity of this devotional panel, *Madonna and Child with St Catherine of Sienna and Angels* (c. 1490; Cat. 149) by Francesco de Giorgio, painted in mixed media, it contains some of his most personal peculiarities. Both the scale of the figures that does not correspond to the existing distance amongst them, and the strongly volumetric construction which — requiring an ample space — remains constrained between the surface of the painting and the honorary drapery that with its decorative linear arabesques closes it off immediately, are contradictory. The powerful relief that is produced by shading, and the geometrization of volumes dissolve between patterns of colours and lines that free the bodies of their weight. The hands of the Virgin, Christ and the Dominican Saint, who presents a flower, are stylized and strongly elongated in gracious gestures. The relation between the figures is ambiguous and lacks warmth, while they also deny contact with the viewer — apart from the figure on the outer right-hand side of the painting who faces us in an almost violent gesture and whose identity of an angel remains problematic. Rather than dealing with interpersonal relations or attempting to find the most effective way to create a devotional image, Francesco di Giorgio seems to entertain himself by trying to solve the formal and decorative pictorical puzzle, that of the real contrast between surface and volume, between lines and colours, in summary that of the necessarily contradictory depiction of three-dimensional reality by imposing an image on a flat surface.

The Lombardian Bernardino Jacobi Butinone (Treviglio, Bergamo, c. 1450 - c. 1507) was also a painter situated between two different artistic concepts, though in less individual terms and with less controversial ideas. The small and elongated panel *The Nativity* (1493, inscribed *"BUTINONS DA TREVILIUS P[INXIT] 1493"*; Cat. 72), painted in tempera and oil, has been linked to an altar-piece in the collegiate church of San Martino de Treviglio, probably produced in collaboration with Bernardino Zenale, and forming part of its predella. Between lateral

149. **Francesco di Giorgio Martini**
Madonna and Child with Saint Catherine and Angels, c. 1490
Mixed media on panel. 62 x 42 cm.

representations of the annunciation to the shepherds, a distant Bethlehem and views of beautiful landscapes, the work depicts a dark rockformation that occludes the space and makes the main theme of the adoration of the Child by Mary and a very old Joseph stand out. Before the interested eyes of the mule and the ox a disproportionately small wingless, kneeling angel, said by some critics to be a donor, kisses the Child, who turns with an agitated movement towards his Mother, seated on the rock. Strong shading applied over the local colours accentuates and defines the volume of the somewhat conventional and little naturalistic figures, while powerful and luminous brushstrokes make the sleeves of the angel iridescent, forming an exceptional passage for the context. The use of these highlights only returns in the rendering of the trees in the landscape. This pictorical and optical treatment of the landscape reveals a partial and, in the end, superficial assimilation of some of the innovations introduced by Leonardo da Vinci in his Milanese work *Virgin of the Rocks* (Musée du Louvre, Paris) that is linked to this traditional and detached work.

Filippo Mazzola (Parma, c. 1460-1505) was a pupil of Francesco Tacconi and part of a family of artists in which his son Girolamo Francesco Maria Mazzola, better known as "Parmigianino", especially stands out, but whom he never trained. He forms a good example of an Emilian craftsman who moves between Lombardic and Venetian influences. His small oil panel *Portrait of Alessandro de Richao* (c. 1491; Cat. 283, with an inscription that reads *"ALEX. DE RICHAO. FI. M.*

72. **Bernardino Butinone**
The Nativity, 1493
Tempera and oil on panel. 46 x 97 cm.

283. **Filippo Mazzola**
Portrait of Alessandro de Richao, after 1491
Oil on panel. 46 x 29 cm.

PAR[MENSIS]. P[INXIT]") shows us the slender and elegant silhouette of a young man cut out against a neutral green background. His garment is of a sober black and is only decorated by the concentric lines of a gold chain and a white collar, and he wears a round hat that does not interrupt the fall of his long hair. This bust portrait shows the sitter, who does not direct his pensive and distant look at the viewer, in three-quarter profile — an originally Nordic formula. It shows signs of the influence of Antonello da Messina, although it lacks the intimacy of the latter's work, and to a lesser extent that of Giovanni Bellini, lacking his feeling for colours and material textures. The arrogant and distant expression of the young man in the portrait here becomes the most notable element of this type of bourgeois portrait that immitated, like its sitters, the manners of the court.

If we move from the individual portrait to the much less usual group portrait, we find the outstanding Lorenzo Costa (Ferrara, c. 1460 - Mantua, 1535). He trained with Ercole de´ Roberti and was in touch with the artistic developments in Florence, which is where he intensified his religious sentimentality. He also worked in Bologna, where this type of painting was highly appreciated, before settling in Mantua in the service of the Este family, converting himself into the successor of Andrea Mantegna as the leading artist of that school. In this canvas, painted in mixed media and dating from his Bolognese period, we are shown the *Group Portrait of the Bentivoglio Family* (1493; Cat. 106), the family in whose service he was together with Francesco Francia, executing palatial decorations. Some of the family members reappear in the Madonna of the Bentivoglio Chapel of San Giacomo Maggiore. According to its inscription, some of the family members are depicted singing a capella: *"I. Sra. Bianca Rangona. II Monsig.re Bentivogli. III. Cantore. IIII. Cantore. V. Sra. Caterina Manfredi. VI. Lorenzo Costa Pittor. VII. Pistano. VIII Sre. Herme Bentivogli. VIIII. Prete delle Tovaglie. X. Sre. Alessandro Bentivogli."*; Giovanni II, the last Bentivoglio governing Bologna until being expelled by Giulio II (1506), and his sons Hermes and Alessandro can be identified among those portrayed; Caterina Manfredi would be the daughter of Francesca Bentivoglio and Galeotto Manfredi. The painter portrayed himself with a beard in the lower left-hand side. In this portrait, a genre which he frequently practiced, the individualities are not very much pronounced and the composition suffers

106. **Lorenzo Costa**
Group Portrait of the Bentivoglio Family, 1493
Mixed media on canvas. 105 x 82 cm.

from the tyranical symmetry he sometimes employed. Yet, the painting strongly evokes the environment of these courts where the lords and their protected artists collaborated very closely.

Bartolomeo Montagna (Orzinuovo, Brescia, c. 1450 - Brescia, 1523) reflects the great achievements of Venetian art and occupies an important place in the Vicenza school. Trained in Venice in the shadow of Giovanni Bellini, with whom he has a very close stylistic and thematic affinity, his production, composed mainly of "sacred conversations" and devotional images, show us his monumental figures — shaped through a rigorous design that passionately seeks the structure below the surface, the bones beneath the flesh, the bare stones below the floor — in bright scenes with implacable white lighting. The critics have ascribed this small oil panel of *St Jerome in the Wilderness* (Cat. 290) — also attributed to Benedetto Rusconi "Diana" — in which we are shown a double image of the saint: studying in meditation — he translated the Bible from the "Vulgata" into Latin — and as a penitent. It presents fragmentary, superficial but very marked similarities to several works by Bellini of very different dates, and makes one think of a deliberate imitation in the form of a *collage*, which demonstrates the devotion towards this saint and the success of Bellini's art.

290. **Bartolomeo Montagna**
Saint Jerome in the Wilderness
Oil on panel. 40 x 28.8 cm.

IV Northern European Painting

When Renaissance art began to develop in Italy at the beginning of the fifteenth century, the rest of Europe remained faithful to the Gothic style and its painting evolved by following the rules of the renovation — *ars nova* — led by the Netherlands, which had an enormous effect on German art. Only towards 1500 did the Northern artists begin to look at the other side of the Alps again. Yet, the plurality of their local interests and traditions led to a reception that was as multiple as the artistic centers that applied themselves to the assimilation of the foreign novelties, and that was not free of attitudes of rejection that were based on different uses of images and the existence of differing modes of perception. Between the Flemish and Italian models German art flourished in a plural manner; diverse were the products of Dürer's and Veit Stoss' Nuremberg and Franconia, and of the High Rhine and Switzerland, whose main exponents were Matthis Grünewald and Hans Baldung Grien. The artists from Swabia and Augsburg, with the Holbeins as leaders, the Danubian Austrians like Albrecht Altdorfer and Wolfgang Huber, or those that painted in Saxen, such as Lucas Cranach, all adopted very diverse rules. A new vision of nature and of history, another conception of the figure of the artist and of the objectives and missions of visual culture, and a new way of understanding the relationship between painting as the craft of representation on a flat surface and painting as the art of representation of a three-dimensional narrative all produced a very special harvest, be it in religious art or in its portrait galleries, of which the Collection shows a varied repertoire.

Austrian painting of the end of the fifteenth century is represented in the Collection by the oil on panel *Portrait of Kunigunda of Austria* (c. 1485; Cat. 8), depicting the daughter of the emperor Frederic III and Eleonor, and wife of the 4th Duke of Bavaria Albert, whom she married in 1487 and whose likeness reappears amongst the funerary statues on the tomb of his brother Maximilian I, executed by Gilg Sesselschreiber for the Hofkirche in Innsbruck. While it is maybe inspired on a lost original by Ludwig Kunraiter, an artist at the service of the Archduke Sigismund, the creator of this version can not be identified with certainty and remains attributed to an "Anonymous Austrian active in the Court of Tirol around 1485", although at times he has been linked to the painter Niclas Reiser of Schwaz, known as the Master of the Habsburg family, active in the court of Innsbruck where Kunigunda spent her childhood. Maybe it concerns a portrait to be presented to a suitor, or for the wedding, judging from the importance given its decorative aspect. It has even been thought that its complex and rich headdress, adorned with pearls, pre-

12. Master Anonymous Nederlandish circa 1520
Portrait of a Man
Oil on panel. 33.5 x 22.5 cm.

8. Master Anonymous Austrian active in the Tyrolean Court
Portrait of Kunigunde of Austria, c. 1485
Oil on panel. 45.5 x 32 cm.

cious stones and small enamel figures, the nudity of which indicates its mundane function, would have belonged to her sister-in-law, the empress Maria of Burgundy. This work constitutes an example of the adaption in an artistically provincial court environment of the novelties of Flemish painting in its emphasis on the elaborated description of features — which in this case naturally are idealized — and of material textures by means of colour and lighting. Also, in this work a preference for the linear and the ornamental remains clear through the importance given to the play of forms in silhouette in order to diminish the volume.

The work *Portrait of a Man* (c. 1520; Cat. 12) by the "Anonymous Dutch artist around 1520" can, despite its later date, maybe serve as a reference. The old attributions of the oil on panel to Jacob Cornelisz. van Oostsaanen, Cornelis Engebrechtsz, to the Master of Alkmaar and to Lucas van Leyden demonstrate to what extent this type of portrait, which seems a bit late for its date, had become generalized in the Netherlands. It had been introduced by Jan van Eyck and Rogier van der Weyden and was put back into fashion by Hans Memling, with the figure in half length — allowing to include the arms in action — and in three-quarter length — endowing the model with more three-dimensionality — against a neutral background in a strong colour. With the figure's dauntless expression and more absent than distanced posture — bearing no relation whatsoever to the viewer — the values of appearance, volume and texture — be it carnations or clothes — in this work dominate the new values of vivacity, immediateness and movement which were added with renewed zeal to the genre's traditional formulas.

The *Portrait of a Man* (c. 1485; Cat. A.891) is also a reflection of this typology, even though with a different atmosphere that is justified by the bourgeois sitter and the painter, Jan Polack (Cracovia (?), c. 1450 — Munich, 1519), who was of Eastern origin — probably Polish — and contributed Bohemian influences to Bavarian painting as he headed an important workshop in Munich. If in his religious painting he shows a passionate and dramatic sense for the themes and forms — which are not devoid of barbarism and would leave traces in Jörg Breu — in his portraits these traces never disappear. This small oil on panel shows us the figure of an older man in bust and three-quarter length on a neutral background of brilliant colouring. The composition is of great simplicity and the appearance caustic, as the details are depicted without an attempt to dissimulate the effects of the passing of time on the face, and the sense of volume is underlined by means of shading and an abrupt brush-stroke that accentuates the sitter's expressive vitality and immediate character. Some of the errors made in the definition of the form, such as the painter's difficulties in correctly reflecting the foreshortening of the most remote eye and in uniting the head with the trunk, bear testimony to the artist's problems in controling the formalistics of contemporary painting and endow the portrait with the charm of the naive and artisan.

The later *Portrait of an Elderly Woman of the Reuss Family* (1524; Cat. 197) presents a greater air and complexity and a more refined character, and was painted by Wolf Huber (Feldkirch, Vorarlberg, c. 1485-1553), a member of a family of artists and painter at the Episcopal court of Passau on the Donau who traveled through Tirol, Salzburg — where he would come in contact with Andrea Mantegna's art — and Augsburg, where he met Albrecht Dürer. He had an individualistic personality within the so-called Donau School and was more than a follower of his contemporary Albrecht Altdorfer — a sharing of interests which is examplified by the luminosity of his landscapes. The old lady Reuss is shown as closed up within herself, although her figure does not lack personality. While she is portrayed in half-length, the movement of her hands has disappeared and her arms serve only as a closure to the composition. She is depicted against the corner of a sober room, while beyond its two windows lies a simplified and likeable mountain landscape painted in a very rough style. This type of composition against an angle formed by two walls and its consequent perspective, which has been constructed in a more intuitive than geometrically rigorous manner, reappears in other

A 891. **Jan Polack**
Portrait of an Elderly Man, c. 1485
Oil on panel. 29.7 x 17.2 cm.

portraits by this painter. This panel that is probably painted in oil offers Wolf Huber's economical, simple and clear language, through which the effect of the whole — of impetuous linear design and soft and delicate colouring — is subordinated to the descriptive detail of the sitter's physionomy and of the textures. This work probably formed part of a diptych as on the back of the panel the family's coat-of-arms with the motto *"MARCESCIT IN OTIO VIRTVS"* (in leisure virtue withers) as well as the date of its execution appear, by another hand than the artist's but maybe that of one of Huber's assistants. It may have accompanied the portrait of the woman's husband or another relative — a certain Stephan Reuss was president of the University of Vienna at the beginning of the century — or maybe it was a devotional picture.

The contemporary work *Portrait of a Man Aged 30* (1525; Cat. 433), attributed with great reservations to Hans Wertinger (Wertinger, c. 1470-Landshut, 1533), also known as "Schwabmaler" (Swabian painter) and a portrait painter still attached to the linear formulas of the late-Gothic tra-

197. **Wolf Huber**
Portrait of an Elderly Woman of the Reuss Family, 1524(?)
Oil on panel. 43 x 32.7 cm.

dition, has a very different and much more representative atmosphere. Wertinger was educated in Augsburg and Landshut and worked in this latter city as a painter and as a designer of xilographies and stained glass windows in the service of the Bavarian ducal family of the Wittelsbachs, although it has been discarded that this portrait may depict the Duke William IV as a consequence of the difference in age and of the barely noble nature of his garments. Despite its inscription *"DO. ICH. BAS. XXX. IAR. ALT. [WV] HET. ICH. DY. GESTALT. 1525"*, which includes the monogram "WV" that appears under a flaming crown in the center and the legend on two pieces of a phylactery that reads *"Wils. so / Wirts."*, the aristocratic sitter remains unidentified.

On an uniform green background on which all these German inscriptions are written, appears the almost half-length figure in three-quarter pose of the noble and energetic sitter who does not lack some melancholical touch and wears an elegant hat, well-groomed garments through which the hilt of a dagger seems to become apparent. He is isolated from the viewer due to the distanced relationship of superiority that is creates by the fact that the picture is presented from above our logical line of vision. The powerful modelling of his face forms a contrast to the lack of volume of the body and to the superficial values of the background that are only

433. **Hans Wertinger** (Attributed to)
Portrait of a Man at the Age of 30, 1525
Oil on canvas laid down on panel. 39 x 34.5 cm.

attenuated by the cutout amulets that float through an impossible space. The *Portrait of a Young Man with a Wreath of Carnations* (c. 1550; Cat. A.892) is also an anonymous panel of likeable court taste. Its carefully tuned colours — the pink of the flowers and the neck, the green of the sleeves and the landscape, the black of the horse and the waistcoat — acquires a dominating significance as it simultaneously creates a powerful contrast with the softness of the composed light — in which some have recognized possible Italian influences — and the geometrical luminous rigidity of the planes of the room's angle in front of which he poses and that is open to the exterior by means of a window, a formula that we have already encountered previously. Its ornament indicates that we may find ourselves facing a matrimonial portrait whose creator, an anonymous painter from Southern Germany, one has not been able to identify once the attempts of attribution to the portrait painter of the Habsburg court, Jakob Seissenegger, have been rejected.

The anonymous *Portrait of Anna Dürer, Wife of Hieronimus Flaischer* (1527; Cat. A.893), identified by its inscription *"ANNA SEIN EHE / FRAU IR EM(?) XXII JAR."*, and the accompanying portrait of her husband — nowadays in the Staatsgalerie in Stuttgart — towards whom the sitter turns her pensive look, is less decorative and more serious. In this oil on panel, which has a very thick and brilliant green

A 892. **Master Anonymous German circa 1550**
Portrait of a Young Man with a Wreath of Carnations
Oil on panel. 35 x 27 cm.

A 893. **Master Anonymous German circa 1527**
Portrait of Anna Dürer, aged 22
Oil on panel. 49.6 x 39.6 cm.

background, appears the vigorous figure of the step-daughter of Endres Dürer, the brother of the painter from Nuremberg, who married the fabricant of hardware products, Flaischer, in 1525. She is portrayed in three-quarter pose and in half-length and has her hands resting around her lap, which may indicate her pregnant state, while the fluid volume of her brocade dress forms a contrast to the descriptive details in other parts in which the linear precision cancels out the form's three-dimensionality. Despite the tentative attributions to Albrecht or to his

295. Hans Muelich
Portrait of a Woman at the Age of 57, 1539
Oil on panel. 71 x 53.5 cm.

brother Hans, the creator of this beautiful work remains anonymous. The *Portrait of a Woman Aged 57* (1539; Cat. 295), an oil on panel, is also part of a pair and is dated and monogrammed *"1539 / HM"* while it carries the inscription *"MEINES ALTERS IM. 57. IAR.".* It is a work by Hans Muelich (Munich, 1516-1573), son of the painter Wolfgang, a follower of Altdorfer and a traveler to Italy — his stay in Rome brilliantly resounds in this early portrait. Soberly dignified yet sympathetic, the lady is seated in a chair against a green wall, the traditionally neutral and superficial character of which breaks the suggestion of the angle and the double surface of a window frame, and whose colour is reflected in the lady's eyes and emerald ring. She is portrayed almost frontally and is constructed through a play of lines, oppositions of colours and textures rather than of volumes, which in her hair-do even loose their three-dimensionality.

Within German painting, Augsburg and Nuremberg were the first cities in which the influence of the Italian Renaissance was felt, although in the art of Ulrich Apt the Elder (Augsburg, c. 1460-1522) it limited itself to producing a new sense of vital abundance. In *The Lamentation* (c. 1510; Cat. 19), a small oil on panel that has been attributed to him, its composition depends almost completely on a Dutch example, maybe by Engebrechtsz. The expression of feeling of the scene inables any intent to logically reconstruct the drama, as demonstrated by St John the Evangelist's move towards the crosses of a Golgotha that he could never contemplate. In the rendering of the objects he does not manage to give them a real sense of volume, despite the dense application of paint in the highlights. A delicate dead Christ forms the center of the painting. Around him the Virgin and the the Holy Maries appear in moved states, with gestures of suffering and in meaningful postures. Even the landscape contributes to accentuate the dramatic atmosphere of the episode, despite its picturesque colouring.

The four large oil panels of a tryptich, the work of a so-called "Anonymous German circa 1515" from the region of Ulm (although previously attributed to Martin Schaffner) and originating from the Premonstratensian monastery of Obermarchtal (Ulm), also show us the continuation of the Northern artistic tradition. On the outer panels appear the episodical depictions of *St Anne with the Virgin and Child and a Donor* (Cat. 266b) and *St Elizabeth Distributing Alms* (Cat. 267b). In the middle The *Adoration of the Shepards* (the inscription on Mary's halo reads *"SANCTA MARIA UND IHS";* Cat. 266a) and *The Presentation in the Temple* (Cat. 267a) complete the work. In these panels an incorrect perspective interferes with the unification of the space below the tree-shaped trilobate arch, on top of which perch *putti* carrying coats of arms, and with a background closed by a golden brocade curtain with ornamental birds sitting on its rails. The very small kneeling donor, the abbot Simon Götz, prays in front of the disproportioned and conventional sculptural figures of the "St Anna Selbdritt". In the other panel a no less sculptural St Elizabeth helps a few dwarfed poor and crippled people. In these two

19. **Ulrich Apt**
The Lamentation, c. 1510
Oil on panel. 44.2 x 35.5 cm.

panels, within the frame of confusing architectonic constructions on a golden background, a crowd of people made to strongly stand out in relief is squeezed in, thus demonstrating that the interest of the artist is centered around the narration of the Evangelist episodes by me-

266a. **Master Anonymous German circa 1515**
The Adoration of the Shepherds
Oil on panel. 159 x 65 cm.

267a. **Master Anonymous German circa 1515**
The Presentation in the Temple
Oil on panel. 159.5 x 65.5 cm.

ans of compository formulas traditional for the time, even though it was based on a *collage* of prints by Martin Schongauer and Dürer without attempting a naturalistic representation. This becomes clear in the Presentation of the well-known wood cut on the same theme by Dürer, in which the high number of figures, many of which are mere extras, are reduced to the absolutely necessary and the proportions are modified: he turns the Child in order to show him to us — more decorously from the front — and forgets the coherent relation

266b. **Master Anonymous German circa 1515**
Saint Anne with the Virgin and Child, with Donor
Oil on panel. 159 x 65 cm.

267b. **Master Anonymous German circa 1515**
Saint Elizabeth distributing Alms
Oil on panel. 159.5 x 65.5 cm.

between figures and the solemn and monumental architectonic frame, which here is transformed into a mere reference of the Temple.

Another German artistic environment, the Saxon, is represented by Lucas (Maler) Cranach the Elder (Kronach, 1472 — Weimar, 1553), son of the painter Hans Maler. He was born in High Franconia and, after traveling through Austria and Flanders, entered the service of the General Elector of Saxony, Frederick the Wise, in Wittenberg. A brilliant, many-sided and versatile painter with great religious doubts, Cranach became a convinced promotor of the reformist ideas of his friend Martin Luther and the most important artist in Northern Germany.

The four oil panels in the Collection together formed the wings of a

110a. **Lucas Cranach the Elder**
Saint Elizabeth with Donor (Duke George of Saxony), c. 1514
Oil on panel. 85 x 31 cm.

111a. **Lucas Cranach the Elder**
Saint Anne with Donor (Duchess Barbara of Saxony), c. 1514
Oil on panel. 85 x 30.6 cm.

medium-size tryptich, maybe flanking a lost painting of the Holy Family, commissioned by the Duke George of Saxony around 1514. On its outside panels were the full-length depictions of *St Christopher* and *St George* (Cat. 110b and 111b), and on the inside panels *St Elizabeth with Donor (Duke of Saxony)* (the inscription in her halo reads *"SANCTA ELISAIBET"*; Cat. 110a and *St Anne with Donor (Duchess Barbara of Saxony)* (identified by its legend *"SANCT ANNA"*; Cat. 111a), both in full length and seated. In front of these two female saints the Dukes of Saxony kneel down in prayer, both depicted in an extremely reduced size and against stairs or a wall, and each with a neutral background.

The two male saints, against a black background that enhances their volume, look at us directly and are examples of Cranach's skillful handling of monumental figures. He emphasizes this monumentality of his figures with the staff and the sword, endowing the works with the quality of portraits, mythological characters of an elevated sensuality or religious

110b. **Lucas Cranach the Elder**
Saint Christopher, c. 1514
Oil on panel. 85 x 31 cm.

111b. **Lucas Crancha the Elder**
Saint George, c. 1514
Oil on panel. 85 x 30.6 cm.

images. The paintings are almost monochrome — red in the case of St Christopher who carries the Child on his shoulders, silver for the saintly knight who treads on the dragon in a relaxed gesture — and thus reinforce his mastering of light and shadow in creating effects of volume, brilliance and textures. On the other hand, on their backgrounds of clear skies the figures of the female saints seem introspective with their measured poses and serene gestures, although they maintain the same characteristics as their male fellow saints. The devotional function of these pictu-

377b-378b. **Christoph Scheller** (Attributed to)
Saint John and Saint Anthony, c. 1520
Carved relief. 118 x 50 cm. each

res, in front of which the sympathetic and aristocratic donors would pray, determined the simplicity of Cranach's painting. Their serious tone may separate them from his more famous works, in which the dramatic narration and the imaginative sense of human nature and the landscape prevail, even though their pictorial qualities may not be less representative.

The art of Bernhard Strigel (Memmingen, c. 1460-1528) has a very different character. He was born into a family of artists known for its production of altarpieces — their important workshop is documented after 1430. Strigel himself participated in important commissions of this kind, such as the paintings in the major altarpiece of the Klosterkirche in Blaubeuren in which he collaborated with the painter Bartholomeus Zeitblom from Ulm. The sculptural elements of the altarpiece were executed by

377a-378a. **Bernhard Strigel**
The Virgin and the Angel of the Annunciation, c. 1515-1520
Oil on panel. 118 x 50 cm. each

Michel Erhart and form one of the most important monuments of the time. Strigel made a name especially as a portraitist, while his principal sitter was the emperor Maximilian, who posed for him several times both on his own and with his family. The *Virgin and the Angel of Annunciation* (c. 1515-1520; Cat. 377a and 378a), oil on panel, places the holy episode in the environment of domestic peacefulness and bourgeois comfort that were prefered in Northern painting. His somewhat unstable, elegant figures, depicted in a long-curved profile, remind of the work of Dieric Bouts. The textural rendering of the cloths follows the good Flemish tradition: the velvet of the Virgin's cloak and the brocade dress underneath it, for example, are sumptuous. On the other hand, a certain Mannerism in the way he treats the abundant materials, as for example the group of parallel folds in the angel's tunic or the arbitrary way in which his cloak folds back, has its origin in the sculpture of the time. The two parts of The Virgin and the Angel of *Anunciation* used to form the outer two wings of a tryptich, while its central panel is lost. The reverse of each panel is decorated with limewood reliefs that have been attributed successively to Hans Thoman and Christoph Scheller, both active in Memmingen and collaborators in the Strigel workshop. The reliefs represent *St John* and *St Anthony* (Cat. no. 377b and 378b) .

The obverse side of the narrow and vertical wings of a tryptich of unknown origin dates from the same period. They are dated thanks to the date (1520 or 1521) that appears on the reverse of the right-hand panel, and were attributed by some critics to the Swabian painter Hans Maler from Ulm (active from 1517 to 1529 in Schwaz, Tirol), and an artisan follower of Bernard Strigel — or maybe even one of his assistants. Yet, for the time being we will have to content ourselves with naming him an "Anonymous German painter from around 1520". Painted in oil on panel and of medium size, the panels depict *The Crucifixion* (Cat. 276) and *Christ in Limbo* (Cat. 277).

Although both compositions are inspired on the engravings "The Great Passion" by Albrecht Dürer, dated in 1511 and 1512 respectively, that have an identical iconography respected by the artist with scholarly application, the final result is far removed from the originals and not only due to the use of a different medium. In the first panel the heroic volume of Christ and the voluminous energy and dramatic gesticulation of the Virgin and St John the Evangelist have been substituted by a very much lengthened and thin body in which the foreshortening has given way to a more sacred frontality and more quiet and reserved figures of measured gestures. Even the symbolical and tragical presence of Adam's skull at the foot of the cross has disappeared. The form of the panel required the painter to break with Dürer's compact composition. As a result, the crucified Christ ended up well above Mary's and St. John's heads. A friendly background with a mountainous landscape and a beautiful fir tree fill up the upper part of the painting. In the story of the descent into Limbo, we find a similar set-up. Adam and Eve are no longer muscular and solid, instead, become elegant and spindle-shaped small figures of simplified anatomy. Christ's strong gesture at the moment of rescueing St John the Baptist turns in a delicate movement that does not require any effort. The divine radiance has given way to a more didactic chorus of souls that stand diffused in the background. Only the phantastic tone of the demo-

276. **Master Anonymous German circa 1520** (?)
The Crucifixion
Oil on panel. 89 x 38 cm.

277. **Master Anonymous German circa 1520** (?)
Christ in Limbo
Oil on panel. 89 x 37.5 cm.

nic creatures has been heightened and they have even taken possession of the frontal plane of the panel through a new infernal figure that does not exist in the original. Obviously, the colouring imposes a different atmosphere on both scenes. The powerful contrast between light and shade of the engravings, which emphasized the dramatism of the episodes of the life of Christ, has been substituted by a combination of tenuous values that is only interrupted by the warm red of Christ's tunic and banner. The vivid intensity of the engravings by the brilliant painter from Nuremburg has been transformed by the hand of the anonymous painter of these panels into a bland and decorative illustration with a friendly tone and a pious and didactic character. In it, Dürer's personal assimilation of the Italian contributions remain diluted with local traditions.

The panel *The Adoration of the Magi* (c. 1520; Cat. 198) was ascribed to the anonymous Master of the Thyssen Adoration who, maybe only because of the use of his engravings, has been related to Wolf Huber. Nevertheless, it cannot be considered an early work by this painter, nor that of one of the members of his workshop. Yet it can be justified that it constitutes one of the most interesting examples of the fusion of the Northern and Italian artistic cultures. Painted in oil, the spaciousness of its perspective and the coordination between the architectonic frame of the half-demolished gate — in a late-Gothical style due to its pointed arches and its pointed, tree-shaped ribs — and the figures that crowd around it has been linked to the Italian Renaissance. The use of a low perspective allows us to identify with St Joseph, the center of the composition in his act of adoration. Nevertheless, the attention given to the colouristic contruction of the scene and the interest shown for the rendering of the optical qualities of the atmosphere — nightly snowfall through which some of its forms are defined impressionistically against the light — bring us back to transalpine environment from where it must have originated, not far from the lyrical and luminous landscape of the School of the Donau. It is this poetic treatment of the environment — which in this case, however, is more artificial than natural — with its marvelous play of light in the clouds and the darkness of a frozen and silent winter atmosphere, that endows this beautiful and original painting with the greatest charm. Above the devotion with which St Joseph contemplates his Son, the courtly elegance of the Magi, the grace of the distant King Balthasar's gesture — a black man dressed in white — or of the anecdotal episodes such as that of the curious Child putting his hand in the present or that of the dog that sniffs the snowy ground, towers this imposing yet charming scenography.

198. **Master of the Thyssen Adoration**
The Adoration of the Magi, c. 1520
Oil on panel. 62 x 44.5 cm.

V The Italian Cinquecento

The Italian sixteenth-century painting, begun by Leonardo, Michelangelo, Rafael and Giorgione, caused the entering of art — which implicated the will to create *works of art* in the modern sense of the word — in the sphere of a new, more extensive and vital verisimilitude that redefined the legacy of Antiquity and the image of nature in a less rigid and more all-embracing way. While the Tuscan-Roman world centered around man and history through a more inventive and subjective medium like drawing, the northern and Venetian art defined a more immediate and direct new mode to tie man and history to their surroundings through the fusion of its images by means of colour and light. Other artistic centers applied themselves to distil these sources with different means, and to re-direct them towards other objectives.

The so-called Pseudo Boccaccino is a figure constructed by the critics and until today remains anonymous (even though he has been identified with the Lombard Giovanni Agostino da Lodi). He owes his name to the resemblance of the works attributed to him to those of Boccaccio Boccaccini from Cremona (active 465-1525), who merged the Ferrara teachings of Ercole de' Roberti and Lorenzo Costa with the Venetian teachings of Giovanni Bellini. Pseudo Boccaccino's style reveals a Milanese origin and an assimilation of the Venetian formulas of the early sixteenth century. This connection is indicated by the pair of

48. Pseudo Boccaccino	**49. Pseudo Boccaccino**
Ladon and Syrinx, c. 1525	*Pan and Syrinx,* c. 1525
Oil on panel. 46 x 36.5 cm.	Oil on panel. 46 x 36.5 cm.

229. **Lorenzo Lotto**
Betrothal of the Virgin, c. 1508
Oil on panel. 45 x 34.5 cm.

oils concerning us and which possibly originate from the decoration of a piece of furniture, maybe a *cassone* or a chest for a dowry. These two small panels with mythological themes, derived from Ovid's "Metamorphosis", show *Pan and Syrinx* (Cat. 49) and *Ladon and Syrinx* (c. 1525; Cat. 48). While their iconographic identification continues to pose problems, it has been thought that in the former the faun Pan appears, trying to conquer the nymph with the harmony of his violin's music, while another young woman flees from the assault of a man, sometimes identified with Daphne and Apollo despite the lack of the precise attributes. In the latter the naiad, as a last resort to escape the obscenities of the pastoral God, appears converted into the reeds with which Pan had fabricated his flute and his syrinx. The river in the front would represent his father Ladon, to whom the nymph had asked for help, although it has also been identified with the young man who seems to be embracing her. Should these readings be correct, we would find ourselves with an ambiguous invitation to chastity because of its functional context. Beyond their reticent meaning, these panels' greatest charm consists of their warm, sensual and pristine atmopsphere — in spite of the anachronism of the *attrezzo* — that is produced by the rustic mythical scenes inserted into a nature that is both fresh and wild, and by the depiction of the landscape that enfolds them in a way that reminds of Leonardo and of Venetian qualities, and which in the end become their most important feature.

Lorenzo Lotto (Venice, c. 1480 - Loreto, 1556) has been considered a self-marginalized Venetian because of his difficult character and his art, which did not conform to the standards of the then ruling Venetian taste. He left Venice at an early date in order to work in more provincial surroundings. His panel *The Betrothal of the Virgin* (c.1508; Cat. 229) already contains some of the characteristics that become more accentuated over the years, above all in his mature work, which is full of a suffering anxiety that reveals his religious stance. This small oil shows us a scene that pertains to the Apocrypha and depicts the election of the mature Joseph as the husband of the Virgin, while his spikenard flowers miraculously. The small dove that sits on the flower comes to confirm the divine intentions. The event is situated in the Re-

131. **Dosso and Battista Dossi**
The Stoning of Saint Stephen, c. 1525
Oil on canvas. 80 x 90 cm.

200. **Pietro degli Ingannati**
Madonna and Child with Saint Agnes in a Landscape
Oil on panel. 60.5 x 85.5 cm.

naissance interior of a sober, heroic and vaulted temple, not in the exterior. A priest on a throne accompanied by two kneeling elders, recognizes the chosen one with ritual unction, while another four pretenders, painted in strong relief, appear to be distressed. A fifth, more angered figure brakes his useless spikenard on his knee, a gesture that seems to be taken from Rafael´s *Betrothal of the Virgin*. A perspective that has its vanishing-point in the background on the right-hand side creates a sense of depth in the chiaroscuro space — emphasized by the illuminated chequered tiles on the floor — and tries to make the static composition of the contained movement more dynamic. The viewer, although standing at the same level as the pretenders, remains more on the outside of the scene, which is clearly marked by a step on the floor and by the white column supporting an arch. Lotto's handling of light and colour is derived from his knowledge of Bellini's, Antonelli's and Dürer's art, while his creation of space seems to be related to the Lombardic innovations in the style of Bramante. The unity of his descriptive realism and his compository extravagance, to which one has to add his strict religious fervour, announce his later nervous subjectivity and his personal disagreement with Roman Classicism and the Venetian sense of complete harmony.

The art of the Emilian Dosso Dossi (Giovanni Luteri; Ferrara, c. 1489-1542) represents Venetian painting's most extreme transformation (brought about by Giorgione and Titian) through a poetic impulse and the use of imagination based on the ideas of Ariosto, and which found an adequate audience in the sophisticated courts of the Este family in Ferrara and the Gonzaga family in Mantua. This small oil of *The Stoning of St Stephen* (c. 1525; Cat. 131), a studio work, has been attributed to Dosso or to his younger brother, Battista, or was considered a work of collaboration. It demonstrates his freedom — even his extravagance — in his treatment of the episode relating the torture of the protomartyr. The dramatic story — presented anachronistically within contemporary surroundings — is lost as it is observed by a girl who keeps the executioners' clothes and is framed by an imaginary landscape splattered with nordic "inventions" (the city of Jerusalem, the rocky and picturesque mountain) that were taken from prints. The archaic and conventional aspects of this picture take on a new dimension thanks to the scheme of vivid and arbitrary colours, of contrasting lighting, of frontal details and the images in the distance. The work's spatial construction is free of the restrictions of a strict perspective and its landscape's lyrical quality — following the tradition of Giorgione — does not cause the unification of elements that are seemingly unequal but the accentuation of the excentric and unexpected aspects of Dotto's personal artistic offer.

In comparison to these individual ventures outside the main interests of the most modern Venetian art, the little known Pietro degli Ingannati (active in Venice, c. 1529-1548) represents the other side of the coin. His panel *Madonna and Child, with St Agnes, in a Landscape* (Cat. 200) is a proof of the success and remaining in force of Giovanni Bellini's old formulas in the field of devotional painting of friendly disposition. The Virgin presents the Child, who grasps a goldfinch, to an inexpressive St Agnes. The scene lacks the emotion that emanates from the psychological relation between the figures — which is demonstrated by their vivid gestures and postures — and from the religious connotations of the theme. The work is superficially resolved as an artisan exercise in the representation of materials and textures, of vivid and intense colours, light and shadow, of the land, constructions and clouded skies — subjects and landscapes in which the artist reaches his greatest achievements.

If by means of the periphery and inertia that lead into opposed direction we move into the most creative center of Venetian art, the figure of Tiziano Vecellio (Pieve di Cadore, c. 1488 - Venice, 1576) represents its highest point and symbolizes the extended life of the

407. Tiziano
Madonna and Child, c. 1545
Oil on panel. 37.5 x 31 cm.

Venetian school of the Cinquecento. After having been under the influence of Giorgione in his beginnings, although he insisted more on relief and on physical immediacy, Titian later incorporated a different type of emotional content and a new sense of movement and colour in the overall pictures, rather than in their individual objects, which endowed his work with light, texture, plasticity and space. The two paintings by Titian in the Collection belong to his mature period before the last changes introduced into his art by the painter at an old age, and represent two of his most beloved genres (together with mythological paintings): religious painting and the portrait.

The small canvas *Madonna and Child* (c. 1545; Cat. 407, although of a debatable chronology, and signed "TITIANVS" on the footstool on which Mary rests her right leg) is in fact the smallest he ever produced and has also been considered a work of collaboration with his son, Orazio (c. 1525-1576). This oil on canvas shows us the image of the Virgin embracing the blond, pink-skinned and pensative Child in a motherly and protective manner, while she directs her gaze at the viewer — maybe even a female spectator of this work of private and feminine devotion — as if demanding his understanding for her posture, her exclusivist conduct by which she refuses to hand over her son. This intimate and private atmosphere is underlined by the soft and closed surroundings that are created by the figures and remain occluded behind these due to the heavy and soft green curtains of the bedroom and the Virgin's covering and expanded cloak. The dense and stable composition of the picture, constructed on the immovable geometric form of a triangle and enhanced both by the horizontal footstool and Mary's firmly placed foot, contributes to this atmosphere. In the same way the warm vermilion of the tunic, the relief and texture which are made to stand out by means of many highlights and which protrudes in relation to the cold blue and green tones, forms a kind of living fortress in the interior of which one could defend the Child that is situated in its center due to the warm pinks and whites of his skin and diaper.

The canvas *Portrait of Antonio Anselmi* (c. 1550; Cat. 404, identified thanks to an old inscription on its reverse that reads "*[Ant]onivs. Anselmvs. ann[i] 38 / 1550 / [T]itianvs F[ecit].*") on a neutral and dark background that reinforces the sitter's volumetry reveals the half-length portrait of a middle-aged and bearded man in a three-quarter profile and wearing a black suit with a fur trimming on top of the white collar. According to the inscription on the back of the painting it would concern Anselmi, Senator of the Most Serene Republic, author and secre-

404. Tiziano
Portrait of Antonio Anselmi, c. 1550
Oil on canvas. 75 x 63 cm.

tary of the Cardinal Pietro Bembo (a collector, and friend and protector of Titian, who was portrayed by him twice and who may have commissioned this work) before he started his personal political activity and whose likeness would again be captured by Tintoretto. The portrait, which does not seem completely finished if judging from the spot that is the hand on a table covered with a mauve cloth, demonstrates Titian's capacity to depict physical features — volume and colour — in great detail and to create a psychological characterization of his models, even of those with a more elusive appearance, which he defines through a visual contact established between them and the viewer. In this particular case, the sitter's gaze combines softness, reservation and disinterest — directing it across to us fleetingly — with a feeling of superiority by psychologically placing us underneath it on an lower plane. Furthermore, this regard has been conferred a vital presence that is underlined by the spontaneous speed of some touches of light and colour.

The qualities of *Portrait of a Senator* (c. 1570; Cat. 399) by Jacopo Robusti (Venice, 1518-1594), named "Tintoretto" after his father's profession of a dyer, can function as a point of contrast in order to take stock of the characteristics of Titian's art and that of his Venetian rival, even though some opinions state that this oil reveals the hand of his daughter, Marietta, who tried to outdo the Master of Cadore by combining his painting with Michelangelo's design and sense of composition and a more forceful dramatic intensity. Although the form is more fragmented — with the exception of the detailed and rich representative drapery that places the figure of this anonymous member of the Republic's Senate in a niche — the suggestion of life in the sitter diminishes as well as our chance to establish contact with him. The play of light on the handkerchief and the hermine fur, of the warm vermilions and the textures of the velvet and brocade, define objects rather than a personality. The latter alludes us between the elements representing the dignity corresponding to his senatorial status — more than to just any individual — and the rethorical gesticulation of his hands. The senator's head remains in the middle distance without connecting properly with his body, inaccessible in a distant space that not even the positioning of his hands manages to liberate. Tintoretto's enormous merits and innovations, which made him into one of the most influential artists of sixteenth-century painting and the representative of a new and alternative method that would be followed even by the individualistic painter El Greco, found a more adequate medium of expression in the eloquent, inventive and complex representation of history than in the more simple and immediate medium of portrait painting.

Despite it lacking the epic quality that Tintoretto had introduced and being resolved in a more decorative and lyrical way, Venetian history painting could be very well represented by the canvas of *The Annunciation* (c. 1570; Cat. 422) by the youngest *caposcuola* of Venice, Paolo Caliari "Veronese" (Verona, 1528 — Venice, 1588), in which the hand of his brother Benedetto has also been detected. The oil painting is organized in a double setting that unites the figure of Gabriel and the spatial plan which is defined by the perspective.

The regard of the viewer is fixed closer-by than the plane of the canvas, far from the development of the scene, below the figure of Mary and on the line of the landscape's horizon that looms through the garden's porch. This recourse, which monumentalizes the relatively small dimensions of the Virgin, contributes to stress the painting's devotional nature but it also keeps us from viewing the story from the visual space of its main figure as it places us in front of a scene that we do not share with the actors. This theatrical aspect and this construction with "drop-scenes" is most pronounced in the scenographic background, from the three-dimensional Ionic marbled columns that, rising on triumphant

399. **Tintoretto**
Portrait of a Senator, c. 1570
Oil on canvas. 118.5 x 100 cm.

pedestals, hide from our view a diaphragm arch in the way of a "pros-
cenium arch", to the emphatic Roman architecture of the majestic palace, which reminds of the Martian Library of Jacopo Sansovino in
which Veronese had painted frescoes. Its complicated positioning on a
much lower plane and even the slight deviation in its vertical lines in
relation to the plumb line on the front plane contribute to create the
impression that we find ourselves in front of a background consisting
of a painted scenographic drop curtain rather than a real brick and
marble structure. The contrasting illumination of the two spaces seems
to require the presence of a "spot light" to cast direct light on the Virgin and that would be more realistic than that cast by the symbolical
divine beam from the Holy Spirit's dove.

The homely setting of the frontal scene is depicted with accessory
elements, such as the sewing basket that stands on a chair — a far-
fetched reference to the veil of the Temple — or the lap dog, the inop-
portune insertion of which from the point of view of thematic, and not
only artistic or compositional necessity would cause the painter many
problems during those years. The elegantly beautiful, warm and moving dancer's figure of the Archangel interrupts this stable and reticula-
ted space. His unexpected presence makes the viewer turn back to the
Virgin, who stands between the heavy folds of her cloak that stand out
in relief, in a calm majestic twisting movement rather than in the agitated act of fearful reaction. In fact, the dynamic effect of her action is
defined by its contrast to the opposing curve of the kneeling-stool and
the moving reflections in the curtain that closes its base, which looks
more like an extension of Mary's figure than an independent object.
With her bodily gesture she closes onto herself by crossing her hands
as a sign of acceptation of her destiny. Instead of chosing one of the
four conventional episodes included in the traditional angelic discourse in the mystery of the Incarnation, Veronese has opted for a synthetic picture that merges all the action in one single moment, from the
initial *conturbatio* to the final *submissio*, which implies the detailed
development of a sequence of stages that were well-known to the
spectators of his times.

With Titian's colourist naturalism, Tintoretto's complex and sometimes bizarre intensity and Veronese's graceful and rhetorical decorative scenography the supreme interests of Venetian art were affirmed
— the artfulness of the natural representation of any reality — and a
point of view established itself that would be essential in the development of Baroque painting.

422. **Paolo Veronese**
The Annunciation, c. 1570
Oil on canvas. 110 x 86.5 cm.

VI European Baroque Painting

European Baroque painting is identified with a new dynamic and complex representation of nature, be it real or imaginary, grand or vulgar. But underneath this apparent unity lie many different ways of seeing — national, social, cultural, religious, functional — that transform the elements processed in works of art.

The traditional and pious renovation combined the formalistic sixteenth-century Roman artistic doctrine with a new verisimilitude based on Venetian colouring and on the dramatic illumination of Roman naturalism, and is represented here by the oil on canvas *The Presentation of the Child in the Temple* (c. 1605; Cat. 84) by Ludovico Carraci (Bologna, 1555-1619). A spacious background of classicist architecture which, without archaeological pretentions, represents the temple of Jerusalem, confers dignity and spaciousness to the narration. Its solemn character is accentuated by the contrast between the light that illuminates the scene from the side and the shadow of the priestly throne and the large pilar that gives way to the Ionic atrium. The Virgin presents the Child — who turns his illuminated face to the crowd — to the old Simeon, whose words in recognition of the Saviour are depicted on the panel shown by the prophetess Anna: *"Ecce positus est hic ruinam et in resu[r]retionem multorum in Israel"* (Lucas, 2, 34). According to the didactic directives of the counter-reformation, processions carrying candles — a traditional reference to the popular feast of the candles — has disappeared and the presentation becomes a premonition of the salvation of humankind, in which Saint Joseph and Anna participate with a reverential expression. It frames a scene that in its hierarchy finds its compository high point in the figures of Maria, Christ and Simeon, who form the focal point for the viewer´s attention.

This line of development of Baroque painting did not reject the teachings of the past and applied them to new interests and formulisms. In Veneto it found favourable grounds even during the development of the most advanced, dynamic and decorative Baroque style. The oil on stone by Francesco Maffei (Vicenza,1605 - Padua,1660) of *The Archangel Saint Michael overthrowing Lucifer* (Cat. 274), related to his *Fall of the Rebellious Angels* (1656) of Venegono Inferiore (Farese), is a perfect example of these directives, although it possibly dates from the sixteen-twenties. Inspired on an engraving by Rafael, the seemingly Veronese colouring and the search for elegant beauty in the fashion of the Cinquecento Mannerists — more so than the later influence of the fleeting brush stroke and movement of Jan Lys, Domenico Fetti or Bernardo Strozzi — give this early work of Maffei a special charm. In it

84. Ludovico Carracci
The Presentation of the Child in the Temple, c. 1605
Oil on canvas. 122 x 91.5 cm.

the luminous and "serpentinate" Archangel seems to be wanting to break out of the fictitious space in his accelerated foreshortening. He spears a frenzied and dark, although no less dynamic, Lucifer within a setting filled with the movement of flames and clouds of smoke that endow the painting with striking contrasts between light and shadow, ugliness and beauty.

The ability of late Baroque painting to synthesize reaches a high level with the likewise Venetian painter Sebastiano Ricci (Belluno, 1659-Venice, 1734), a fervent traveller and a crucible of many different contemporary and historical influences. The canvas *Magdalena comforted by Angels* (c. 1694; Cat. 339) was executed before he reached his most developed style after his return to Venice at the beginning of the eighteenth century, unites the freshness of brush-stroke of his master Sebastiano Mazzoni, the Parmasan grace of Correggio, the sense of volume of the Bolonese Classicists and the emotional rhetoric that leads from Ribera to Luca Giordano. Three angels stand out against an orange-coloured sky of day-brake. Their postures embody the sentiments that Ricci wants to transmit to the viewer: veneration, the following of the right example and compassion. The Saint, exhausted after prolonged prayer that has, however, not faded her sensual beauty, is being sheltered in the lap of a compassionate third angel. The symbols of her life and her ascetic meditations — the back of the cave, the bed of esparto grass, the book of prayers, the teachings and the scull — surround her

274. **Francesco Maffei**
Saint Michael Overthrowing Lucifer, 1640-1660
Oil on stone. 80 x 75 cm...

339. **Sebastiano Ricci**
Saint Magdalen comforted by Angels, c. 1694
Oil on canvas. 147 x 112.5 cm.

languidly. They remain on a secondary plane next to a seraph who turns his face, full of pain and suffering, towards the Saint. A small angel shows the seraph and the viewer a whip, counteracting the main diagonal that forms the axis of the composition of the scene by forming a second, slanting and three-dimensional compository directive.

The most important figure in seventeenth-century Flemish painting is beyond any doubt Peter Paul Rubens (Siegen, 1577 - Antwerp, 1640), connoisseur of Italian, Spanish and British art, courtier, diplomat, scholar and hedonist, versatile genius and head of an enormous workshop. With him the tradition of sixteenth-century Northern Naturalism reaches its peak. He assimilated the teachings of antiquity and the Italians of the past and present and elevated Flemish art beyond the obvious or the uninspired copying of the art of other countries, reaching the objective of a naturalistic, lively and imaginative art that ennobles everyting it involves.

This elevated, dynamic, naturalistic rhetorical and theatrical tone appears in the complex oil *St Roch as the Patron of the Plague-stricken* (c. 1623; Cat. 353), which is attributed to him. This oil sketch on panel is dedicated to the mission of St Roch as the protector of the plague-stricken; a Christ figure — between judge and the resurrected — appears

353. **Rubens** (Attributed to)
Saint Roch as Patron of the Plague-Stricken, c. 1623
Oil on oak panel. 64.3 x 49.5 cm.

surrounded by clouds in front a church entrance and shows the kneeling Saint, dressed as a pilgrim, the living objects of his care, while an angel points at a certificate for beatification that marks his future role: *"Eris in peste patronvs"*. Below, sheltered under the arch of a cellar or subterranean, a group of ill people raises its regard and arms, begging for his role as an intermediary. Although it has been related to an altar piece dedicated to St Roch at the church of St Martin in Aalts, commissioned by its brotherhood to the studio of Rubens in 1626, this link cannot be made with certainty due to the differences between the two works and because this popular work has been itself copied and modified on several occasions. The critics have never reached an agreement as to the autography of this small oil either, as its quality and the level of its finishing are uneven — as evidenced by the mere contrast between the upper and lower parts, as well as by the retouchings (as in the case of the large upper arch). As a result, we may find ourselves in front of a variation inspired by Rubens.

A work that is definitely a Rubens is the large canvas *The Virgin and Child with St Elizabeth and the Infant St John* (c. 1618; Cat. 349), in which, with Rafaelesque echos of *The Pearl*, the quiet conversation between the Virgin — in a state of meditative introspection — and the Child — who presents the sheep of his future offer — are shown to us. A young St John playfully rides on the back of the symbolical animal, thus contributing to a friendly reading of the theme. On the animal's back lies an abandoned cross, while St Elizabeth holds her child and contemplates the central scene with feeling interest. Judging from the number of reproductions, copies and engravings that are based on it, this is a very successful painting that unites meditation — Latin verses that specify the Christian meaning appear on some of the engravings — and pleasure in an intimate family scene. The children have even been identified as portraits of Albert and Nicolas, two of the painter's sons.

Easier to discern than the pious associations and the references to the innocent and endeering scene with children and family life is the outstanding quality of this oil, one of the best executions of this theme produced by Flemish painting. The closing and covering positioning of the two women above the children accentuates the intimate and domestic nature of the image while the rounded figures are balanced by the grey mass of the columns that all have different shafts. The horizontal bands on the right delineate a type of "frame" above St Elizabeth's head — while the clouds do the same above Maria's head — and, from the wavy pink veil at the Virgin's feet, closes the tridimensional diagonal

349. Rubens
Virgin and Child with St Elizabeth and the Infant St John the Baptist, c. 1618
Oil on canvas. 151 x 113 cm.

that counteracts and enlivens the centripetal set-up of the scene. In the center is the foreshortened and feeling head of the Child. The variety of textures and tones, from the wrinkled wool and the austere drape of St Elizabeth to the intense vermilion of Maria's tunic, from the former's withered complexion to the mother-of-pearl-like and smooth skin of the latter or the children's rosy and smooth softness, reinforce the sensation of true reality in all its plenty that is captured by Rubens' canvas; he even allows himself to introduce a sensual element by unveiling the round bossom of the Virgin. The feminine, child-like, animalistic, moral, material, artificial and natural beauty seems to enliven the whole painting as if the representation of the beauty of reality — after finding and imagining it — would constitute one of the artist's main objectives.

Motivated by the production in the Italian and Flemish centers, the Spanish school of painting of the seventeenth century with the generation of Zurbarán, Alonso Cano and Velázquez reached a high point in its manifold naturalistic interests as it followed a path that was started in Italy by the Valentian Jusepe Ribera, and which would be completed by the Sevillians Bartolomé Esteban Murillo and Juan de Valdés Leal. Despite having been forged at the same hearth, the difference in character between these artists and the different social and functional circles in which they moved and for which they worked lead them to seek individual modes of expression that could be adapted coherently to the representation of the various types of images that they were asked for, and that would be a natural development from their own artisitc intentions and their personal concepts of what they thought an artist ought to be and do.

Francisco de Zurbarán (Fuente de Cantos (Badajoz), 1598 - Madrid, 1664) followed the most traditional course for a painter as a craftman producing work in series, preferably at the service of monasteries and parishes which identified the art of painting with the production of images, pious narratives and, above all, "images" in the strictest sense of the term: sanctuaries of a devotional nature. His enormous canvas *Christ on the Cross* (c. 1630; Cat. 447) with all its virtues and limitations adequately represents the directives of his earliest explorations, after his stay in Llerena and the execution of his cheap and hasty series of episodes and saints for the Dominicans of San Pablo el Real in Seville. Although it has been compared with the splendid *Crucifixion*, signed and dated 1627, of the oratory of the sacristy of the preachers (The Art Institute, Chicago) — an exceptional work for its quality and intense emotion — the parallels and differences between these two paintings point

447. **Zurbarán**
Christ on the Cross, c. 1630
Oil on canvas. 214 x 143.5 cm..

at very diverse objectives. Both canvases show the figure of Christ on the cross with the *titulus* ("*Iesvs Nazarenvs Rex Ivdeorvm*") in Latin and Greek and four nails, on a dark background that emphasizes the solitude and the tridimensional corporality — as if it were a sculptured image with a rounded shape. This iconographic formula, defended by some commentators of the gospel and by erudite artists such as Francisco Pacheco, implied a more frontal and stable depiction of the image of Christ, not resting one foot on the other and putting one leg slightly forward. In the *Crucifixion* in Chicago, the dead Christ carries the whole of his weight on the support, thus accentuating the sense of inert yet triumphal weight, while he inclines his head into the penumbra of his flank in the serene and dignified posture of death. In the Christ of Pedralbes, however, Christ is depicted in a state of agony. While still alive, his mouth is open, his head turned and he raises his eyes toward the Father. His body tenses in a spiral movement that forces his anatomy and distorts the image, which seeks the expression of a moment filled with pathos. In spite of the energetic drawing and the contrasting lighting, the appearance of relief and the sensation of the textures of the flesh and the materials, and the magic of the colouring and the tone of the incomprehensible mystery have been largely diluted. The feet become disproportionally large, as if a viewing from afar and below were maybe foreseen, or as if their mass would want to anchor itself on the support to a too dynamic Christ, reinforcing his points of support. Christ's vital twisting movement defies the correct rendering of the legs and arms and, by baring his hip, destroys the magical and untouchable plotting of verticals and horizontals that makes the Christ in Chicago a masterpiece. Reality described as the image of a self-sufficient and impassible still-life gives way to the narration of an historical scene — failing so often in Zurbarán's art, as he only knows how to solve this in a conventional and lifeless manner.

As the prime artist at Philip IV's court, Diego Rodríguez de Silva y Velázquez (Seville, 1599 — Madrid, 1660) fundamentally took up the genre of public and private portrait painting, which he would execute for the enjoyment of the members of the royal family or for its shipment in series to the different European courts that requested a visual record of their relatives or alies. His late *Portrait of Maria Anna of Austria, Queen of Spain* (1655-57; Cat. 416) offers us the bust of the second wife of Philip IV and introduces us to the yet-unsolved problem of the mechanics of the production of portraits by the painter in his studio at the Madrilenean royal palace. Is it a preparatory study still lacking the

416. Velázquez
Portrait of Maria Anna of Austria, Queen of Spain, 1655 - 1657
Oil on canvas. 66 x 56 cm.

last touches that would give it corporality and would enliven the forms that are basically still two-dimensional? Or is it a qualified replica in which the elaborated description of the royal face makes that which goes beyond its mere contours into a second priority? His cousin and wife, who is only little over twenty years of age, turns her eyes towards us from her more removed three-quarter pose with a less direct and energetic look than usual — think of the canvas in which she appears in full lenght and with ample pomp at the Prado Museum — while the strenght of her personality transfers itself into a more fidgety and wavy hair-style. Maybe we find ourselves in front of a more familiar and less showy work — as is the case with other half-length portraits — that had to be sent to some aristocratic "servant", a member of the royal family far removed from the court, and in which less importance was given to its representative character and to the pictorial effort of the, also functional, art of Velázquez.

Compared to the Flemish and Spanish artistic production, which in their formalistic characteristics were strongly indebted to the Italian outlook, the great Dutch art remained more independent. Political and religious causes, which defined different interpretations of common subjects and new genres and that, above all, followed different intentions based on other concepts of the mission of art, guaranteed the maintenance of specific characteristics of artistic schools, which made Dutch art one of the most interesting and original of seventeenth-century Europe. While Rembrandt, Frans Hals and Jan Vermeer represent the high points of history — of portrait and genre painting, of art with a capital A — a whole group of artist tended to specialize themselves in the so-called minor genres, such as landscape and still-life painting. The specific characteristics of the Dutch vision of reality and the forms employed in its artistic representation — art as a mirror of nature rather than its pure representation — were combined very successfully.

With the older Jan van Goyen and the younger Meindert Hobbema, Salomon Jacobsz. van Ruysdael (Naarden, c. 1600 — Haarlem, 1670), member of an important family of artists, ocupies the most important place amongst Dutch landscape painters. He focused his artistic activity in the most important center for this genre, Haarlem, and shared Van Goyen's and Hobbema's interest for naturalistic rendering of the local landscape — as opposed to the imaginative school of Rembrandt. In their paintings the unification of light and space, by means of the use of colours that have the effect of blending together, became the prime objective alongside detailed representation.

His late panel *Sailing Vessels Moored near a Village* (1660; Cat. 361, signed with the monogram "S RV" on the central boat), which in the stricted sense should be called a "seascape", exemplifies the novelties introduced by Ruysdael to perfection. They have come to be identified with the structural, monumental and "classical" type of Dutch landscape painting that is free of accessories. A low horizon that does not coincide with the human figures, dotted around the boats and the shore, delineates a set of abscissas together with the hulls of the boats and the roofs of the huts, and allows for a great elaboration of the sky, which is filled with heavy clouds of contrasting and varied colours. These mark some diagonal movements, lines of force that overpower the rest of the representation. Secondary vectors

361. **Salomon Jacobsz. van Ruysdael**
Sailing Vessels moored near a Village, 1660
Oil on panel. 46.1 x 63.5 cm.

that deeply penetrate into the space are defined by the foreshortened
and zigzagging piece of land and the diagonal placing of the sailboat
and the rowing boat. The artificial masts of the sailing boats form a
contrast to the horizontal positioning of nature, as if they were ordina-
tes of a system of geometric coordinates that structure the whole. The
ephemeral moment in which the clouds in their constant movement
form a instantaneous figure and with their colours reflect the rays of
sunlight remains captured for the infinity of visual memory. The at
once serene and dynamic, superficial and three-dimensional narrative
of the work takes us to the farthest removed line of the horizon, where
everything that is immediate, measurable and pertains to everyday life
is reduced until it dissolves into the infinitely minute and where all of
observable reality dissappears from our view. The atmospheric phe-
nomena and their reflections, which dissolve the limits of the reality
of the sky and the calm sea, however, are not only visually recogniza-
ble physical objects that are susceptible to being molded thanks to the
painting's aerial and atmospheric perspective. Rather, they become
eloquent objects that are able to create a number of different, and not
necessarily optical, sensations in the viewer that are impregnated with
smell, temperature, humidity or touch, or even some full of all-enve-
loping emotions — anouncing features of the eighteenth-century poetic sensibility.

Even though Venetian painting of the eighteenth century is known and appreciated more for its formal virtuosity, its brilliant colouring, compository focus on ornamentation and the attractiveness of its minor genres, it never abondoned the field of religious painting. While artists like Antonio Pellegrini or Jacopo Amigoni and even Pittoni, after the lessons learned from Ricci and Luca Giordano, joined the current that sought a likeable novelty and the most sophisticated complexity, Francesco Bencovich and, above all, Piazzetta opted for a less superficial, profounder and more intense renovation that would reach its brilliant peak in the work of Tiepolo.

Giovanni Battista Piazzetta (Venice, 1683-1754), who was younger than Ricci and whose life story and interests were very different from the latter's, represents the versatility of the Venetian School. *The Sacrifice of Isaac* (1712-14; Cat. 318) was painted shortly after he returned from Bologna, where he had completed his training with Giuseppe Maria Crespi. It is a sample of his characteristic use of chiaroscuro and of the play of warm and earthy colours, as well as of his structural feel-

323. **Giovanni Battista Pittoni**
The Rest on the Flight into Egypt, c. 1725-1726
Oil on canvas. 108 x 135 cm.

ing for plastic forms, which he employs in order to obtain a profound emotional intensity that finds its perfect compository vehicle in the zigzagging movement of the forms. The painting is also an example of Piazzetta's ability to simultaneously organize figures and feelings in opposing directives. In this splendid and moving canvas Isaac's masculine beauty is offered to the viewer as an abandoned victim at the knife held by Abraham. This powerful and aggressive old man, who energetically brandishes the weapon and in a fatherly fashion reaches out for the body of his son, seems to urge the feminine angel for a rescueing intervention. The old biblical story finds a new dimension as classical myth through the work's emotional load, tactile plasticity and dynamic and vibrant composition, which is very coherently structured.

In comparison to his contemporary, Giovanni Battista Pittoni (Venice, 1687-1767) represents the decorative and likeable tendency, the elegance, fresh colouring, ease and Arcadian sentiments of which have been associated with the French Rococo. His *Rest on the Flight into Egypt* (c. 1725; Cat. 323), painted from a very low perspective, submerges us in a religious episode of an intimate tone and tender disposition. The Child, who seems to lightly signal to the viewer, shares his gracious appearance with his parents — rather than with the cherubs, who only function to balance the composition — and this childish gesture,

318. **Giovanni Battista Piazzetta**
The Sacrifice of Isaac, 1712 - 1714
Oil on canvas. 100 x 125.5 cm.

half-way between the harpocratic sign and the more familiar act of suc-king a thumb — requires our silent presence. The not quite lateral but intense lighting softens the forms, while the natural elements — the far-away landscape and the trees — and anecdotal details — the walking stick and water bottle for traveling -, the subdued colours of the clouds and the blue and yellow tones of the clothing cool down and de-dra-matize the effect of this oil. Its iconography, the vigil of the Child-God on an ashlar stone (interpretable as an altar of sacrifice), could have been imbued with darker and more transcendental meaning had anot-her, more formal treatment been used.

Giambattista Tiepolo's (Venice, 1696 — Madrid, 1770) youthful canvas *The Way to Golgotha* (c. 1728; Cat. 395), of such complex and chaotic composition, wonderfully represents the air of renovation that such a brilliant painter could blow into the art of his master Piaz-

395. **Giambattista Tiepolo**
The Way to Golgotha, c. 1728
Oil on canvas. 79 x 86 cm.

398. **Giandomenico Tiepolo**
The Expulsion from the Temple, c. 1760
Oil on canvas. 104 x 195 cm.

zetta by incorporating the "grand manner" of Veronese and Ricci, clarifying the colouring, opening spaces, emphasizing movement and enrichening the composition. In contrast to the calm of the handcuffed thiefs and the Holy Women, in which the elegance and colour of the soldiers also stand out, and the lightness of the trees and the solidity of the far-away town, the scene itself zigzags along a deep diagonal towards the still remote and elevated Calvario. Two executioners pull the cross along in that direction while the body of Christ twists towards us, flinging his emotional gesture at us from the red colour of his tunic. On the right St. Veronica duplicates the image of the Lord. This play of reiterations and counterpositionings structures a complex and simple tragical scene, the center of which opposes and frames the loud crowd and the contained pathos of the lonely and isolated figure of Christ. An apparent formal lightness and a powerful, both religious and human emotion fuse to give new life to this old theme.

The teachings of the father, alongside his virtues and his more limited personality, remain clear in this early *The Expulsion from the Temple* (c. 1760; Cat. 398) by Giandomenico Tiepolo (Venice, 1727-1804). There is a greater simplification in the composition, a more reduced variety of tones, shadows, textures and emotions, and a lesser sense of volume and of space despite the architectonic rhetoric in the background. The intensity of the story is deluted by anecdotal episodes or by a somewhat forceful theatricality to which the painting's extremely low perspective and the importance given to the optical illusion of the objects on the front plane contribute, while it does not exclude a comical element. This element, which is personalized by the man who, despite holding on to the table, falls onto the floor, in the end manages to conceal the destiny of divine indignation, the beautiful woman that asks for mercy while showing a money bag.

The eighteenth century showed the proliferation from Milan to Naples of genre painting which had penetrated Italy in the seventeenth century from the Flemish world with the *babocciate* of Pieter van Laer and the *arti di Bologna* of the incisive eye of Annibale Carraci. This multiplicity caused its diversification, its very varied tones and expressive intentions, to the point of dissolving the frontier between this genre and others, as evidenced by the paintings of Amoroso, Longhi, Ceruti or Traversi.

The two small canvases *Girl Sewing* (Cat. 5) and *The Tapestry Seller* (c. 1720; Cat. A.888) are by Antonio Amoroso. Active in Rome, a pupil of Giuseppe Ghezzi and influenced by Rembrandt's disciple Bernhard Keil (known in Italy as "Monsù Bernardo"), Amoroso painted religious works and portraits, although he has reached greater fame for his monumental treatment of genre scenes. In these two paintings the feeling of intimacy of an immediate and dignified reality predominates. The treatment of light and the dark background enhance the painting's tactile and pictorial value and endow the scenes with a tone of surpri-

A 888. **Antonio Amoroso**
A Boy Selling Tapestry, c. 1720
Oil on canvas. 41 x 32.5 cm.

5. **Antonio Amoroso**
A Girl Sewing, c. 1720
Oil on canvas. 41 x 31 cm.

A 889. **Pietro Longhi**
Portrait of a Lady
Oil on canvas. 48.3 x 35.6 cm.

sing intimacy, namely that of the young woman embroidering in her frame, engrossed in her work without affording us so much as a glance or a word, or that of the smiling young man who does look at us and offers us his merchandise without hiding his feelings.

Pietro (Falca) Longhi (Venice, 1702-1785) applied himself to depicting the social life of the bourgeoisie in the enlightened city of Venice. His paintings have left behind a chronicle of the period — almost a local chronicle — through an eye more liberated of prejudices than that of the "modern moral themes" of William Hogarth, and parallel to the literary work of Goldoni. In his small *Portrait of a Lady* (Cat. A.889) the limits between the portrait of the bourgeoisie (the table and the drapery testify to the elements representative of the tradition in modern portrait painting), the chronicle of the going out for an evening walk and the trivial and anecdotal episode become faded. The lady, wearing a three-cornered hat and holding a fan, moves towards the door from within homely surroundings that reduce the old symbols of representation to the category of objects of an every-day and comfortable decoration. However, the lady does not pose for the portrait painter but turns towards the yellow spot of the canary that escaped from its cage and is a little less interested in this banal feat than is the tiny company dog that reacts astoundedly to this unusual and insignificant event.

In Lombardy Giacomo Ceruti (Milano, 1698-1767) painted portraits and still-lifes and paintings of beggars — which gave him the diminutive nickname "Pitochetto" — simultaneously. Within this latter category his large canvas *Group of Beggars* (1736; Cat. 86), commissioned by the known collector the Marshal von Schulenberg, stands out. The portrait of the three beggars is executed with an amplitude proper to greater genres, and through the elaboration of its volumetry and details elevates the picture of these three marginal characters in formalistic terms. The absence of a moralistic tone adds to the visual objectivity of the representation, which is enhanced by the neutral tone of the ocres and browns and by its independence of the viewer. Two old men are resting; one, who is standing and leans on a stick, hides his face from us; the other, who is sitting, conveys an image of dignified and serene confidence which produces comprehension and sympathy rather than pity or contempt; the distrust is a result of the interior of his own world, of the old woman who looks at the latter dryly and suspiciously while she clutches her miserable clothing.

The tone becomes very different again in *The Fainting* (Cat. A.890), an oil possibly executed in Rome after 1749 by the Napolitan Gaspare

86. **Giacomo Ceruti**
Group of Beggars, 1736
Oil on canvas. 130.5 x 95 cm.

Traversi (Naples, 1732 - Rome, 1769). Under the Austrian viceroyship and the future kingdom of Charles III this revalued painter drank from the fountains of a tradition that went back to Ribera and Preti and that was revived by Solimena and Francesco De Mura. This inspiration on seventeenth-century painting has formalistic origins — a striving for luminous effects, a preoccupation with descriptive details, thick brushstrokes — that were meant to affect the content, but that also contemplated small, both serious and ridiculous episodes of bourgeois life with imagination and exemplary objectivity. A young lady has fainted and the mistress of the house is taking her pulse while an old man supports her head and takes advantage of the situation to peep down her décolté. Although this canvas has been related to the *commedia dell'arte* and some of its most characteristic figures — the beloved young lady, the match-making woman and the old lover — the farcical and theatrical tone shines in its absence. Rather, a subtle irony that does not lack moralistic notes trickles through the realist image at the margin of our look or our associations.

Naturalism would reach one of its high points in Italy, from Gaspar

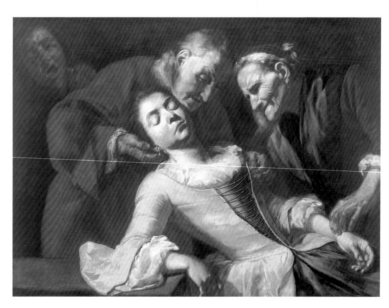

A 890. **Gaspare Traversi**
The Fainting, after 1749
Oil on canvas. 74.2 x 100.4 cm.

77. Canaletto
Il Bucintoro, Venice, c. 1745-1750
Oil on canvas. 57 x 93 cm.

van Wittel in Naples to Giovanni Pannini in Rome and Luca Carlevariis in Venice, with the genre of the *veduta*, the urban view, in which the description of the cityscape and its small inhabitants was mixed in a new way for the pleasure of both travelers seeking to collect *souvenirs* and demanding art collectors, as much in the past as today. And beyond doubt the Venetian cityscape, the culmination of the imagination and memory of tourists of all times, has found its most conspicious and famed representatives in Canaletto and in Guardi, without forgetting the younger Bernardo Bellotto. Despite apparent similarities in their themes and techniques, the options chosen by Canaletto and Guardi rather testify to the infinite number of possible approaches of the same reality offered by a period situated between the reign of Charles III and Romanticism and that out of tradition was open to new interpretations and experiences.

Antonio Giovanni Canale "Canaletto" (Venice, 1697-1768) was the son of a set designer and himself decorator of operas by Scarlatti. During an early stay in Rome he took the instrument of the craft by antonomasia, the perspective, to its utmost consequences in order to create a fictitious reality based on the scenery of a theatre or to mold three-dimensional reality — colourist and luminous architectonic spaces and planes or water. This was useful for obtaining effects that had never been seen before, such as the idealization of non-existing landscapes or the preservation of the image of a real environment. "Canaletto" strived for the objective work of a *vedutista* with a topographical tendency, who portrays the adorned and festive or every-day old city of

105

the Serene Republic with a craftman's exactitude and with reverential faithfulness. His *Il "Bucintoro" in Venice* (c. 1745; Cat. 77) captures the annual picture of the celebration of the marriage of the Doge and the Sea, which took place on the day of Ascension and in which the head of the government embarked his representative galley in order to get married on the waters of the Laguna. Innumerable gondolas surround the duke's ship and dot the frontal plane of the painting, more as scattered spots of colour than as representations of human activity. Nevertheless, it is the sky and the front of the facciata a mare — from the church of La Salute, slowly erring through the Ceca and the Biblioteca Marciana to the Ducal Palace and the Prison and the *campanile* of San Marco, through its planes rather than behind its mass — that are the true and double protagonists of this painting.

The perspective, a scientific structure of the empirical perception of a merely visual reality, controls the elements of the coloured picture that reaches our retina with geometrical rigor and allows them to be transmitted onto a canvas. Yet, renouncing to the whims of the capricious set designer, "Canaletto" denies his technique its own ability to transform reality. He does not use the perspective as a means to focus the center of attention of his scene, to deform an image or to emphasize the far background (the Grand Canal has disappeared as such), but instead makes it into the instrument of the personal point of view of the observer who dominates the view and bends the image to his or her will. He only uses the perspective to objectively control the city that reaches us in the afternoon's lighting and which imposes its presence upon us permanently, as if he would want to properly place the tourist, passive viewer and traveler.

Francesco Guardi (Venice, 1712-1793), a virtuoso of light and colour as his brother-in-law Giambattista Tiepolo and a prodigious artist for the instant and delicate touch of his brush, chose another way to depict Venice. As he was more inclined towards a pictoresque and capricious view and was more imaginative and manipulating, he engaged himself in a suggestive and imaginative representation based on the infinite number of plays of lighting and colour — to which his amazing and stimulating agility contributed — of spacious views or of unusual locations and details he made us discover in Venice. In a way, his *View of Piazzetta di San Marco towards la Laguna* (Cat. A.897) combines these two types of cityscapes. Horizontally extended beyond the enormous and popular Piazza di San Marco are the Piazzetta — inverting its rigid planimetry — and, behind the two columns that support the Lion of St Mark the Evangelist and St George, without forming an interruption in the canal, the Palladian church of San Giorgio Maggiore, which is partly concealed by a boat. On the left the afternoon sun illuminates the façade of the Ducal Palace while on the right the Library of San Marco remains in a shaded area that is only disturbed by touches of light that dot the outer balustrade. The space between these two buildings is crowded by small figures that situate the viewer within his real perspective and fill up the space without attracting our attention.

Once again, it is the city, still depicted from the view of the individual, that dominates the, maybe more obsolete, unusual, contingent and less eternal picture. The combinations of colour and of light and shadow promote more phantastic visions and include an element ignored by "Canaletto": feeling. The images are not only the products of visual memory but also of the states of mind that are associated with perceptive or imaginary experiences or with real or fictitious situations. They are memories of individual and transmittable experiences that can be shared. In comparison to "Canaletto's" elaborate and precise chorography, Guardi revealed images, taken from scenes of reality, as emotional experiences.

A 897. **Francesco Guardi**
View of Piazzetta di San Marco towards la Laguna,
Oil on canvas. 69 x 86.5 cm.

List of Works

5. AMOROSO ANTONIO. *A Girl Sewing,* c. 1720. Oil on canvas, 41 x 31 cm.

A 888. AMOROSO ANTONIO. *A Boy Selling Tapestry,* c. 1720. Oil on canvas, 41 x 32.5 cm.

6. ANDREA DI BARTOLO. *The Way to Calvary,* c. 1415-1420. Tempera on panel, 54.5 x 49 cm.

7. ANGELICO, Fra. *The Madonna of Humility,* c. 1433-1435. Tempera on panel, 98.6 x 49.2 cm.

19. APT, Ulrich. *The Lamentation,* c. 1510. Oil on panel, 44.2 x 35.5 cm.

A 896. BARNABA DA MODENA. *Madonna and Child with two Angels,* c. 1374. Tempera and gold on panel, 51.5 x 37.6 cm.

45. BICCI DI LORENZO. *Christ on the Cross with the Virgin and Saint John,* c. 1430. Tempera on panel, 75.5 x 31.4 cm.

46. BICCI DI LORENZO. *Announcing Angel,* c. 1430. Tempera on panel, 69.3 x 30.8 cm.

47. BICCI DI LORENZO. *Annunciate Virgin,* c. 1430. Tempera on panel, 69 x 31.9 cm.

48. BOCCACCINO, Pseudo. *Ladon and Syrinx,* c. 1525. Oil on panel, 46 x 36.5 cm.

49. BOCCACCINO, Pseudo. *Pan and Syrinx,* c. 1525. Oil on panel, 46 x 36.5 cm.

50. BOCCATI, Giovanni. *Saint Sabinus conversing with Saint Benedict,* 1473. Oil on panel, 27 x 35.9 cm.

72. BUTINONE, Bernardino. *The Nativity,* 1493. Tempera and oil on panel, 46 x 97 cm.

77. CANALETTO. *Il Bucintoro, Venice,* c. 1745-1750. Oil on canvas, 57 x 93 cm.

84. CARRACCI, Ludovico. *The Presentation of the Child in the Temple,* c. 1605. Oil on canvas, 122 x 91.5 cm.

85. CENNI DI FRANCESCO DI SER CENNI. *The Madonna of Humility,* c. 1375-1380. Tempera on panel, 76.6 x 51.2 cm.

86. CERUTI, Giacomo. *Group of Beggars,* 1736. Oil on canvas, 130.5 x 95 cm.

103. COSSA, Francesco del. *Saint Claire,* c. 1470-1472. Tempera on panel, 27 x 8 cm.

104. COSSA, Francesco del. *Saint Catherine,* c. 1470-1472. Tempera on panel, 27 x 8 cm.

106. COSTA, Lorenzo. *Group Portrait of the Bentivoglio Family,* 1493. Mixed media on canvas, 105 x 82 cm.

110a. CRANACH, Lucas the Elder. *Saint Elizabeth with Donor (Duke George of Saxony),* c. 1514. Oil on panel, 85 x 31 cm.

110b. CRANACH, Lucas the Elder. *Saint Christopher,* c. 1514. Oil on panel, 85 x 31 cm.

111a. CRANACH, Lucas the Elder. *Saint Anne with Donor (Duchess Barbara of Saxony),* c. 1514. Oil on panel, 85 x 30.6 cm.

111b. CRANACH, Lucas the Elder. *Saint George,* c. 1514. Oil on panel, 85 x 30.6 cm.

122. DADDI, Bernardo. *Madonna and Child,* c. 1340-1345. Tempera on panel, 84 x 54.8 cm.

131. DOSSI, Dosso and Battista. *The Stoning of Saint Stephen,* c. 1525. Oil on canvas, 80 x 90 cm.

149. FRANCESCO DI GIORGIO MARTINI. *Madonna and Child with Saint Catherine and Angels,* c. 1490. Mixed media on panel, 62 x 42 cm.

152. GADDI, Taddeo. *Nativity,* c. 1325. Tempera on panel, 35.5 x 37 cm.

3. GIOVANNI DA BOLOGNA. *The Coronation of the Virgin and four Angels,* c. 1380-1390. Tempera on panel, 45 x 21.7 cm.

A 897. GUARDI, Francesco. *View of Piazzetta di San Marco towards la Laguna.* Oil on canvas, 69 x 86.5 cm.

197. HUBER, Wolf. *Portrait of an Elderly Woman of the Reuss Family,* 1524(?). Oil on panel, 43 x 32.7 cm.

200. INGANNATI, Pietro degli. *Madonna and Child with Saint Agnes in a Landscape.* Oil on panel, 60.5 x 85.5 cm.

A 889. LONGHI, Pietro. *Portrait of a Lady.* Oil on canvas, 48.3 x 35.6 cm.

227. LORENZO MONACO. *Madonna and Child enthroned with six Angels,* c. 1415-1420. Tempera on panel, 147 x 82 cm.

229. LOTTO, Lorenzo. *Betrothal of the Virgin,* c. 1508. Oil on panel, 45 x 34.5 cm.

274. MAFFEI, Francesco. *Saint Michael Overthrowing Lucifer,* 1640-1660. Oil on stone, 80 x 75 cm.

248. MASTER OF FORLÌ. *The Deposition,* c. 1300-1305. Tempera on panel, 19.7 x 13.3 cm.

A 894. MASTER OF THE DOTTO CHAPEL. *The Last Judgement,* c. 1290. Tempera on panel, 17 x 18.3 cm.

A 895. MASTER OF THE DOTTO CHAPEL. *The Crucifixion,* c. 1290. Tempera on panel, 17 x 18.2 cm.

198. MASTER OF THE THYSSEN

ADORATION. *The Adoration of the Magi,* c. 1520. Oil on panel, 62 x 44.5 cm.

8. MASTER, ANONYMOUS AUSTRIAN active in the Tyrolean Court. *Portrait of Kunigunde of Austria,* c. 1485. Oil on panel, 45.5 x 32 cm.

266a-266b. MASTER, ANONYMOUS GERMAN circa 1515. (a) *The Adoration of the Shepherds.* (b) *Saint Anne with the Virgin and Child, with Donor.* Oil on panel, 159 x 65 cm.

267a-267b. MASTER, ANONYMOUS GERMAN circa 1515. (a) *The Presentation in the Temple.* (b) *Saint Elizabeth distributing Alms.* Oil on panel, 159.5 x 65.5 cm.

A 892. MASTER, ANONYMOUS GERMAN circa 1550. *Portrait of a Young Man with a Wreath of Carnations.* Oil on panel, 35 x 27 cm.

A 893. MASTER, ANONYMOUS GERMAN circa 1527. *Portrait of Anna Dürer, aged 22.* Oil on panel, 49.6 x 39.6 cm.

276. MASTER, ANONYMOUS GERMAN circa 1520 (?). *The Crucifixion.* Oil on panel, 89 x 38 cm.

277. MASTER, ANONYMOUS GERMAN circa 1520 (?). *Christ in Limbo.* Oil on panel, 89 x 37.5 cm.

12. MASTER, ANONYMOUS NEDERLANDISH circa 1520. *Portrait of a Man.* Oil on panel, 33.5 x 22.5 cm.

283. MAZZOLA, Filippo. *Portrait of Alessandro de Richao,* after 1491. Oil on panel, 46 x 29 cm.

290. MONTAGNA, Bartolomeo. *Saint Jerome in the Wilderness.* Oil on panel, 40 x 28.8 cm.

295. MUELICH, Hans. *Portrait of a Woman Aged 57,* 1539. Oil on panel, 71 x 53.5 cm.

303. NICCOLÒ DI TOMMASO. *Madonna and Child with six Saints,* c. 1362-1367. Tempera on panel, 87 x 39 cm.

318. PIAZZETTA, Giovanni Battista. *The Sacrifice of Isaac,* 1712 - 1714. Oil on canvas, 100 x 125.5 cm.

321. PIETRO DA RIMINI. *The Nativity and Episodes from Christ' s infancy,* c. 1330. Tempera on panel, 17.2 x 19.7 cm.

323. PITTONI, Giovanni Battista. *The Rest on the Flight into Egypt,* c. 1725-1726. Oil on canvas, 108 x 135 cm.

A 891. POLACK, Jan. *Portrait of an Elderly Man,* c. 1485. Oil on panel, 29.7 x 17.2 cm.

339. RICCI, Sebastiano. *Saint Magdalen comforted by Angels,* c. 1694. Oil on canvas, 147 x 112.5 cm.

349. RUBENS, Peter Paul. *Virgin and Child with St Elizabeth and the Infant St John the Baptist,* c. 1618. Oil on canvas, 151 x 113 cm.

353. RUBENS, Peter Paul (attributed to). *Saint Roch as Patron of the Plague-Stricken,* c. 1623. Oil on oak panel, 64.3 x 49.5 cm.

361. RUYSDAEL, Salomon Jacobsz. van. *Sailing Vessels moored near a Village,* 1660. Oil on panel, 46.1 x 63.5 cm.

377a-378a. STRIGEL, Bernhard. *The Virgin and the Angel of the Annunciation,* c. 1515-1520. Oil on panel, 118 x 50 cm. each.

377b-378b. SCHELLER, Christoph (attributed to). *Saint John and Saint Anthony,* c. 1520. Carved relief, 118 x 50 cm. each.

395. TIEPOLO, Giambattista. *The Way to Golgotha,* c. 1728. Oil on canvas, 79 x 86 cm.

398. TIEPOLO, Giandomenico. *The Expulsion from the Temple,* c. 1760. Oil on canvas, 104 x 195 cm.

399. TINTORETTO. *Portrait of a Senator,* c. 1570. Oil on canvas, 118.5 x 100 cm.

404. TIZIANO. *Portrait of Antonio Anselmi,* c. 1550. Oil on canvas, 75 x 63 cm.

407. TIZIANO. *Madonna and Child,* c. 1545. Oil on panel, 37.5 x 31 cm.

A 890. TRAVERSI, Gaspare. *The Fainting,* after 1749. Oil on canvas, 74.2 x 100.4 cm.

416. VELÁZQUEZ. *Portrait of Maria Anna of Austria, Queen of Spain,* 1655 - 1657. Oil on canvas, 66 x 56 cm.

422. VERONESE, Paolo. *The Annunciation,* c. 1570. Oil on canvas, 110 x 86.5 cm.

433. WERTINGER, Hans (attributed to). *Portrait of a Man at the Age of 30,* 1525. Oil on canvas laid down on panel, 39 x 34.5 cm.

447. ZURBARÁN. *Christ on the Cross,* c. 1630. Oil on canvas, 214 x 143.5 cm.

SCULPTURES

S95. *Head of a Prophet,* 1250 - 1300. Limestone. Height: 38 cm.

S96. *Seated Prophet,* c. 1180 - 1185. Limestone. Height: 125 cm.

S97. *Virgin and Child,* c. 1250 - 1275. Sandstone. Height: 181 cm.

S98. *Virgin and Child with Moses and the Burning Bush,* 1310 - 1330. Limestone. Height: 155 cm.

S99. *Virgin and Child,* 1300 - 1350. Polychromed wood. Height: 101 cm.

S100. *Standing warrior,* c. 1450. White stone, with remains of polychromy. Height: 86 cm.

S101. *The Assumption of the Virgin,* 1450-1500. Alabaster. Height: 40.7 cm.

S102. *The Dead Christ,* c. 1230 - 1250. Polychromed poplar. Height: 174 cm.

ELECTA

Phototyping
EFCA, S.A.

Lithography
Lucam

Printing
Aries, S.A.

FUNDACIÓN COLECCIÓN THYSSEN-BORNEMISZA
Publishing coordinator: *María del Mar Borobia Guerrero*

Photographs
José Loren
Villa Favorita